CH00487132

the taste of a place
corfu

Published in 2002 by
Wittersham Publishing
PO Box 39705
London
W4 4WA

Set in Optima and Gill Sans Light 9/11.

Design and layout by 2g Ltd.

Printed and bound by Proost, Belgium

A catalogue record for this book is available
from the British Library

ISBN 0-9542692-0-9

contents

Introduction

Do you find food on holiday is always a bit of a disappointment?

Is choosing a decent taverna a bit of a hit-and-miss affair?

Are the shops frustrating?

Do you end up drinking the same, boring wine every day because at least you know it is drinkable?

Well, this book will take all the guesswork out of eating and drinking in Corfu.

Inside, you will find:

- What to expect when you buy food, from the everyday necessities like bread to unusual purchases such as *sykópitta*. (What's that? Turn to page 20 to find out.)

- The criteria to use when choosing a taverna, along with suggestions of some to try (plus the opportunity for you to nominate your own favourites via our website).

- A culinary tour of Corfu Town, which follows the locals to the best shops and the finest produce.

- Easy-to-cook recipes that make the most of local ingredients, whether you have a fully equipped kitchen or just a knife.

- An introduction to Greek booze, from super plonk to some serious wine.

It's all Greek to me...

To help you make yourself understood when shopping or eating out, this guide includes key Greek words and phrases, transliterated into the English (Roman) alphabet. To use them correctly, you'll need to put the emphasis on the right bit of each word; when applicable, we've used acute accents to show which vowel sound needs to be accentuated. For example, *kaliméra* (which means 'good morning') is pronounced kali-**mer**-a.

In some chapters, particularly those about buying ingredients, we've also included names as they appear when written in the Greek alphabet. This should help you recognise foods and wines by their Greek labels when you're out shopping.

For those of you keen to learn more, Lonely Planet publishes a good Greek phrase book.

Corfiot cuisine

What is typical Corfiot cooking? Take a walk through any of the island's resorts and you will see there are enough Indian, Chinese and burger takeaways for the average visitor to spend two weeks without tasting anything authentically Greek, let alone Corfiot.

In some ways, this is not surprising. When mass tourism first began, tavernas stuck to the standard tourist menu available throughout Greece and, by and large, holidaymakers were happy with that. Tastes change, though. What was once comfortingly familiar eventually became a tad dull and repetitive; hence the proliferation of food outlets from other countries.

Secondly, cooking in Corfu has its roots in the home, rather than the restaurant. Classic Corfiot dishes such as *sofrito* and *bourthéto*, which now appear on some taverna menus, are both examples of 'one pot' cuisine. This style developed because most Corfiot housewives didn't have modern stoves or hot-plates until the mid-20th century, so they would pile meat and/or vegetables into a pan and leave it to stew all day in a wood-burning oven – often the one belonging to the village bakery, a tradition that continues to this day.

A history of good food

Both *sofrito* and *bourthéto* highlight aspects of Corfu's culinary heritage and the way the islanders still like to eat today.

Historically, Corfu occupied a key position, both military and mercantile, in a region that was fought over for centuries. As empires rose and fell, so Corfu changed hands. It was occupied by the Venetians for 600 years, but never by the Turks. Thus spices such as cumin – a mainstay in the Middle East – don't make it to the table. Instead, Corfiot cooks love to use fresh herbs to flavour their food. *Sofrito* is the perfect example: where 'veal' (actually young beef) is slowly braised with large amounts of parsley, garlic and vinegar.

The exception to the spice rule is ground red pepper: both hot and mild varieties appear in *bourthéto*, a fish stew with a hot paprika sauce that is unique to Corfu – even the other Ionian islands don't use this spice. There are several theories as to how it came to be introduced but, whatever the explanation, during the Venetian rule, significant amounts of pepper began to be imported.

Bourthéto is a corruption of the Italian word 'brodetto', meaning soup or broth. Whilst Italian words – or versions of them – are very much in evidence in the Corfiot dialect, one couldn't say that Corfiot cooking is particularly Venetian. This is probably because the Venetians kept a feudal system in force on the island, which meant the majority of the locals lived in poverty. Cooking was very much a question of making do with what little you had got. However, pasta is popular in Corfu: there even used to be a macaroni-making factory close to the airport. Corfu's legendary greenness is also due to the Venetians, who bribed Corfiots to plant olive trees and so keep their empire supplied with olive oil. Other Italian credits include the introduction of the tomato.

What of other rulers? Well, the French stayed in Corfu only long enough to build somewhere really nice to sit, drink, and watch the world go by: The Liston, an elegant arcade of cafés in the centre of Corfu Town, which is modelled on Rue de Rivoli in Paris. And as for the British who governed Corfu between 1815 and 1864 – their sole contribution to the culinary repertoire was ginger beer. Apparently you can still sip it while watching the cricket in the bars of The Liston. Another place to imbibe freshly made ginger beer is in Old Perithia, a village just below Mt Pantecrator in the north of the island, at the taverna called O Foros.

Soul food

Corfiot cooking is not just influenced by history. Religion, both in terms of feasts and fasting, also plays a vital role.

Easter is the most important religious event of the year in Corfu – indeed the whole of Greece. One of the most famous of Greek salads, *taramosalata*, is a Lenten dish eaten on Clean Monday, the start of Lent. Traditionally, fish and meat are not eaten during Lent, although shellfish are allowed.

The Good Friday service, *epitáphios*, is a very solemn occasion with a funeral procession of Christ's bier decorated with flowers; it is followed on Saturday night by the service of the Resurrection, when everyone goes to church bearing an unlit candle. At the first stroke of midnight in the darkened church, the priest lights his candle from the eternal flame burning at the altar and proclaims 'Christ is risen', to which the congregation replies, 'truly He is risen'. Everyone lights their candles, repeating this incantation to one another as fireworks explode and church bells peal – and then hurries home to break their fast with the traditional meal of an egg, lemon and lamb intestine soup.

On Easter Sunday, the family feast traditionally centres on roast spit lamb: before the advent of European Union regulations, non-Greeks often found themselves disconcerted by the spectacle of roadside slaughters of this Paschal lamb.

Other celebratory foods will include hard-boiled eggs, an Easter symbol dyed red to represent the blood of Christ. Young and old alike will use them to play an egg-bashing game similar to conkers, where the victor is the one that doesn't end up with egg on their hands. Strictly speaking, the two 'contestants' should utter the words 'Christ is risen/truly He is risen' as the eggs crunch together, but the religious aspect of the game seems to have fallen by the wayside. If not being bashed to bits, red eggs are sometimes hidden inside a special bread made at Easter time, called *foghatsa*. This is a sweet and spicy plaited loaf, similar to hot cross buns in flavour and texture, and is eaten from Sunday morning onwards.

Whatever the occasion, Corfiots are discerning and cautious eaters. And that means the quality and range of produce is good: you just need to know where to look for it. So in the following chapters we take a look at where to get the best Corfiot food, both in tavernas, and in shops and markets.

Eating out

The best tavernas — and other possibilities

Tavernas

To review of all the tavernas, snack bars and restaurants on Corfu would require a tome the size of Encyclopaedia Britannica. It would also be inaccurate: establishments regularly change hands, chefs leave, or their marriages hit the rocks along with the standard of cooking. Popularity, ironically, can also have adverse consequences: the kitchen may struggle to cope with the increase in demand and then start to cut corners. (This is actually a pretty similar pattern to other European countries, such as the UK, where the average length of time a restaurant business remains in the same hands is a mere 18 months.) And with large industrial units in Athens churning out slurries of bilious pink taramosalata to satiate the appetites of the millions of tourists who visit Greece every year, where do you go if you want a handmade version of the dip? How do you choose where to eat, when you have only got two weeks to find the perfect place for dinner? Well, here are some criteria to apply when making your choice.

Look for a good location

Crystal cobalt waters, hazy blue mountains, the shade of an olive tree and a glass of chilled something to hand: the ambience and surroundings of your meals out are almost more important than the food itself. There are two bays in north-eastern Corfu that epitomise this: Aghios Stephanos and, further south, Agni. Despite their popularity, they have not yet fallen victim to thoughtless development. Even more amazingly, the tavernas in both of them all serve great food; in peak season you may have to wait a while, but this is hardly a hardship.

At Aghios Stephanos, four tavernas are strung along a charming bay, popular with flotillas. Named Eucalyptus, Kaparelli, Galini and Kochili, each has their own devotees.

Agni used to be accessible only by boat or on foot, thus adding romance to the beauty of the place. Unfortunately there is now a road, though it's in a dreadful condition – long may it remain this way, so that visitors will continue to arrive by sea. If you arrive by boat, don't worry about your navigation skills when it comes to mooring: you'll be providing quiet entertainment for onlookers, and anyway, staff at the tavernas will tie up and anchor your boat for you. There are three tavernas to choose from – Nicholas, Agni and Toula – all of which serve good food in different styles.

Of course, tavernas don't have to be by the sea to have a great location. So if you like people-watching, consider the Rex, behind The Liston in Corfu Town.

Agni
Agni

If sophisticated taverna food and a good wine list are your priorities, then head here. The priciest of the three tavernas in Agni bay, its house specials include fresh Albanian mussels in an alcoholy, garlicy sauce – have them as a starter and you will want them as a main course too, as these mussels are some of the plumpest, juiciest molluscs in the Mediterranean. And even if the thought of pickled octopus conjures visions of vinegared tyre rubber, try it at Agni. Its version is a revelation: meaty, delicately flavoured and delicious.

Where: beachfront, furthest left as you face the sea

Tel: 06630 91142

Open: May to end Oct

Eucalyptus
Aghios Stephanos

So named because of a large eucalyptus tree growing to one side, this taverna has the advantage of fronting directly onto the shingle beach at Ag. Stephanos, making it ideal for those with young children. People praise their *souvlakia* (skewered chunks of meat on bamboo sticks); grilled to order, the meat is tender and seasoned with the herb *rigani* (see page 38) and lemon juice.

Where: the road to Ag. Stephanos comes down into the bay; when it bends right to follow the shoreline you'll see the taverna straight in front of you

Tel: 06630 82007

Open: May to October

Galini
Aghios Stephanos

Galini was one of the original buildings in Ag. Stephanos, servicing the passing caiques which, until 25 years ago, were the easiest way of getting around the coastline. In those days you would call in by boat on your way to a deserted and inaccessible-by-road beach. The owner would bustle out to wave and greet you, shout what was on the menu for lunch that day – perhaps grilled octopus or swordfish – and you would make your order, returning three hours later suitably sunburnt and thirsty. It is still very popular with yachts, and the menu is a lot more wide-ranging and sophisticated than 20 years ago: these days you can have prawn cocktail and steak, if that is your wish.

Where: heading towards Kerasia, on the right after Kaparelli (see below)

Tel: 06630 81492

Open: May to end October

Kaparelli
Aghios Stephanos

A bustling taverna with an extensive menu, Kaparelli is situated next door to Galini (see above); the seating areas for both overlook the harbour and the jetty, and are ideal for a romantic, waterside evening watching a full moon rise over Albania just a few kilometres away. Try their moussaka or fish *mezethes* (savoury titbits).

Where: the road turns right and runs south through Ag. Stephanos; Kaparelli is the first taverna you'll come to, about 50m along the road

Tel: 06630 81511

Open: May to October

Kochili
Aghios Stephanos

Kochili may not have the best position in Ag. Stephanos as it is set back from the sea front, but it more than makes up for this with its daily specials. These include *bianco* (made with firm-fleshed white fish, potatoes, garlic and lemon), whitebait when in season, and tiny triangular *tyropitta* made with filo pastry and a feta filling flecked with parsley. Their *lahano dolmades* – stuffed white cabbage leaves – are also delicious and much better than the more usual stuffed vine leaves.

Where: the last taverna on the right as you drive through Ag. Stephanos towards Kerasia

Tel: 06630 81522

Open: May to October

Nicholas
Agni

Nicholas has the nicest position on the beach at Agni, tucked on the right-hand side as you look out to sea. It has been a favourite with visitors for years, not only because of the extensive *mezethes* menu (which allows a family to share a meal but still eat what they like), but also because of the boundless energy and enthusiasm of Peracles – son of the original Nicholas – and his staff.

Where: on the right hand side of Agni bay, as one faces the sea

Tel: 06630 91136

Open: May to October

Rex
Corfu Town

This is one of the posher and more expensive tavernas around; in fact. technically it is not a taverna at all, but an *estiatorio* (restaurant). It has an Art Deco-style interior with mirrored walls, and linen tablecloths rather than the more usual paper ones. The food, too, is at the posh end of the taverna repertoire. Specials change daily and might include rabbit with mushrooms, fresh, fried sardines – crisp skinned with lovely moist flesh – or pork with celery. This is a generous portion of pork fillet in a lemon sauce with *sélino* – the celery herb, rather than the corrugated vegetable loathed by legions of school children. The standard menu is extensive, including a wide range of pasta dishes.

Where: 66 Kapodistriou Street, Corfu Town

Tel: 06610 39649

Open: all day, all year

Toula's
Agni

A favourite with many of the expats on the island, this taverna's style of cooking is happily positioned somewhere between its two neighbours at Agni: good Greek food that includes some more unusual dishes, such as a prawn risotto.

Where: the first taverna after turning left onto Agni beach

Tel: 06630 91350

Open: May to October

Check the menu for local specialities

More and more tavernas serve local dishes or have cooks doing their own thing in the kitchens. Of these, the following are particularly worth looking out for.

Alonaki Bay View Taverna
Alonaki Bay, Aghios Mattheos

A popular spot with Ag. Mattheos locals, who congregate here for Sunday lunch. The taverna is on a very small cliff top that overlooks Alonaki Bay (a hedge screens the drop, except for a 2m gap where two tables have a view of the sea below – prime position, unless you have small children). Tables are scattered on concrete plinths under the shade of olive and pine trees – a bit like a picnic park – but there are lots of nooks and crannies stuffed with flowering pot-plants, so you don't feel crowded by your neighbours. Free-range hens and a minah bird merrily calling 'yassoo' at passer-bys add extra character. The taverna serves a local version of *bourthéto*, the fiery, Corfiot, peppered fish stew. Though usually made with white fish, in this area locals use eels from the nearby lake; larger eels are served grilled with the herb *rigani* and bay leaves. Specials of the day might include *bianco* (fish with lemon, garlic and potato), a vegetable casserole of courgette, green beans and carrot, tender casseroled rabbit with small whole onions, and *pastitsatha*, a pasta and meat ragout.

Where: Halicouna, nr Aghios Mattheos. After Ag. Mattheos, travel south out of the town. Follow the signs to Alonaki Beach, and have faith: it is a long and winding road. You will pass two tavernas before finding signs to the Alonaki Bay View, which is on the right before you reach the lake

Tel: 06610 75872

Open: all day every day in the tourist season; weekends only during the winter

Etrusco
Kato Korakiana

The best Italian restaurant on the island and, if you want somewhere special, *the* place to go. The menu is extensive, mixing the unusual and familiar in antipasti such as octopus carpaccio, a selection of hams, or deep-fried julienne vegetables and kalamari in tempura batter served with a cumin-spiced tomato salsa. There are several seafood pasta dishes, whilst the pappardelle and duck with black truffle makes a rich and delicious change if you are suffering from a surfeit of tomatoes with every meal. Portions are very generous, so don't expect to work your way through all of the courses Italian-style. The wine list features good Greek wines – the chef-owner is an enthusiast who believes that Greek wines now have the consistency and quality to make starting a cellar a worth-while proposition.

Where: travelling towards Corfu Town on the main road through Dassia, turn right at the Kato Korikiana junction (opposite the Eko petrol station). The restaurant is 150m up the road on the right-hand corner as the road sweeps left into Kato Korikiana

Tel: 06610 93342

Open: Easter until October; evenings only; booking essential

George's
Almiros Beach, Acharavi

George's taverna overlooks a very sandy beach, which at this end of Acharavi doesn't get too crowded. He learnt to cook from his mother, who ran the taverna before him and who is still very much in evidence, and creates his own variations on Corfiot specialities such as *sofrito* – George doesn't use vinegar (which he thinks is a horrible addition) but Metaxa brandy instead. His wife, Sophia, also cooks. One of her specialities is a seafood pasta with prawn, kalamari and mushrooms; the fish is all bought direct from local fishermen, and really is fresh, rather than freshly defrosted. At the end of the tourist season – i.e. at the beginning of autumn, when evenings start to become chilly – they serve hearty vegetable soups which are meals in themselves. And if you have overdosed on chips (by day nine of your holiday, I defy you not to feel daunted at the prospect of yet another chip) you will be delighted to discover that both George and Sophia are happy to dish up boiled potatoes on request.

Where: coming from Kassiopi, travel 0.6km past the Texaco garage on the right. Look for three small signs sign on the left by a junction – the top one says George's – and turn right. At the next T-junction turn left, then follow the road round to the right and down to the beach. The road swings right again; the taverna will then be 30m ahead of you

Tel: 06630 63753

Open: from Easter to end Oct

Follow the Greeks

Tavernas that remain open all year do so because they rely on local – rather than just tourist – trade. They tend not to be in beautiful locations, but more typically are situated on a village high street, or close to a residential area.

Capricorn Taverna
Kassiopi

Capricorn is owned and run by Kostas and his Chilean wife Lydia. He cooks, she does front of house. Their business has been in three different locations over the last 20 years; but wherever they go, the locals follow. On cold March evenings (depending on weather conditions) cuttlefish stew and *hórta* (see page 41) will be on the menu. For those that don't feel quite that adventurous, pork roll is a good bet and available year round. Other seasonal dishes include beef soup and grilled horse mushrooms, and the *tyropitta* are delicious – the secret, apparently, is a dash of ouzo and a sprinkling of chopped dill mixed in with the feta filling.

Where: Seki Bay, between Kassiopi and Perithia, 1.6km beyond the 'leaving Kassiopi' sign if you're travelling from Kassiopi

Tel: only Greek spoken!

Open: all day, all year

Nakos
Shell Petrol Station, Ropa Valley Road

Shell is onto a winner here: 24-hour grocery stores be damned! The family that manages the service station also runs a thriving taverna that looks as if it has grown considerably over the years. The service-station entrance leads onto a back room with two open fireplaces, which itself leads into another dining room overlooking a garden and play area. It is popular with Corfiots and expats alike, particularly in the winter months. It serves very good grills and has a wider-than-average range of vegetables, such as fried pumpkin, to choose from.

Where: at the southern end of the road that longitudinally bisects the Ropa Valley. Coming from Corfu Town, pass the Aqualand theme park on your left, then turn right at the next roundabout. The Shell petrol station is about 100m along the road on the right

Tel: 06610 94255

Open: evenings year round; weekend lunch times, closed Sundays in winter

The Pumphouse
Acharavi

Despite the lengthy menu – including a children's section – the food here is always freshly prepared. The Pumphouse is strong on casseroles: chicken and vegetable stew, rabbit in wine sauce, rooster Corfu-style, and leg of lamb baked with tomato and cheese are just some of its speciality dishes. Another attraction is the very large, wood-burning stove in the dining room – very pleasant when it is pouring with rain on a miserable November day.

Where: facing the roundabout in the centre of Acharavi, on the Mt Pantecrator (not beach) side of the road

Tel: 06630 63271

Open: all year

Stamatis Taverna
Viros

Should you get lost trying to find Stamatis, your solace will be that you will find yourself in a very pretty, unspoilt bit of Corfu (you may even find the holiday home of your dreams). The taverna is a hut with a beer garden shaded by a large orange tree. It does not look very much, but by night it is transformed into a jolly experience, full of Corfiots out to enjoy some very good food. The menu is only in Greek, but the staff speak English (the owner's wife is Scottish). Chef Spiros, the son of Stamatis, likes to experiment. Menu appearances have included individual chicken pies, and layered aubergine and spicy sausage baked with a mashed-potato topping. Live folk music often adds to the ambience, and it is extremely popular: get there early – early for Greeks is 8.30-9pm – at weekends.

Where: take the Benitses road south out of Corfu Town. After passing the Metro Cash & Carry supermarket on your left you will see a poorly positioned signpost to Viros on the right. Turn into this road and follow it for 1km until you reach a three-pronged fork. Ignore the one signposted to Viros, and take the lower of the two remaining prongs straight ahead on the main road. One hundred metres further on, there is another higher / lower road split. Take the higher. You will end up in a dead end, faced by Stamatis

Tel: 06610 39249

Open: evenings only. closed Oct / Nov (which is when Spiros likes to concentrate on making the taverna's wine)

Thomas Grill Room
Karrousades

As the name suggests, this taverna only does grills – and jolly good ones too. It has recently made concessions to the occasional tourists who make it to this hill-top town and the menu is now available in English. Not that this is really necessary, as diners can see the grill on one side of the dining room and point to what they fancy. In addition to the usual *souvlaki* and chicken, in spring they also serve the local delicacy *kokoretsi* – lamb offal such as heart, kidney and lights – spit-roasted.

Where: as the road from Roda sweeps gently right, turn left at the sign to Karrousades. Once you have passed the post office on the right, 200m up the hill, look for somewhere to park; the restaurant is another 200m further up, parking outside is impossible as the road is very narrow

Tel: only Greek spoken!

Open: all year, evenings only

Yannis
Garista, Corfu Town

This family-run establishment is a classic example of how tavernas used to be before the advent of mass tourism. And the reason it has stayed traditional is because its clientele are primarily from the suburb in which it is located. You can of course order from the menu, but it is better to do as the Greeks do: go into the kitchen and inspect the pans. You will be given a slip of paper on which to take note of what you fancy. Dishes include stuffed tomatoes, *pastithada, stifado* – all the favourites.

Where: travel south out of Corfu Town on the Alkinou road (which runs behind and parallel to the coast road); Yannis is on the right at the southern end of the road

Tel: 06610 31066

Open: all year, evenings only

Get fresh

It might seem self-evident, but if you are looking for good, freshly prepared food that is a little out of the ordinary, you'll have to avoid bars and restaurants with plasticised menus and pictures of the dishes they serve, football matches showing live that evening, and huge signs saying 'Full English Breakfast' – unless of course that is what you are after.

And fresh food also means a bit of a wait. At all the tavernas mentioned in this chapter, you will have to wait whilst food is prepared, or go without if availability is limited. Look at it this way: if your chicken doesn't go under the grill until you've ordered it, you can be sure your tzatziki won't have been made in Thessaloniki.

There is particularly likely to be a wait for seafood. The Olive Press, on the west coast at San Stephano (tel: 06630 52137, evenings only) asks customers to ring in advance if they want freshly caught fish, while the fish tavernas in Petriti and Boukari (one of the best tavernas is Spiros Karidis, tel: 06620 51205) will expect you to choose from the catch of the day. Need advice? Go for the spiny lobster – those caught on this stretch of the southern Corfiot coast are said to be the best on the island.

Alternative eats

If a full meal isn't what you're looking for, try some of these other options.

Psistaría

Psistaría, or grill-rooms, specialise in charcoal-grilled meat but, sadly, traditional ones are not that common anymore. However, they do still thrive anywhere with a high turnover of people, such as the bus station or the New Port in Corfu Town, and the Paleocrastritsa / Kassiopi junction in Gouvia. *Psistaría* serve baby pork *souvlakia* dripping lemon juice and oil, with a doorstop hunk of fresh bread — so much nicer than a beef-burger for a snack on the run.

Ouzeria

Bars with the description *ouzeria* (ouzo bars) above the door will have been around from the days before tourism and are splendid places for snacking on *mezethes*. There are several scattered around the Old Port and The Liston in Corfu Town. Since Greeks don't drink without eating, it's easy to accompany your drink with a little plate of something: try *saganaki* (fried cheese) or pickled octopus.

Kafeneia

Traditional *kafeneia*, or cafés, don't score highly on the comfy-chair scale, but can't be beaten for a mule-kick of caffeine and a *pásta* (a pastry cake) at the start of your day. Even the smallest village will have a *kafeneion*: look for a nondescript shop-front where there will be at least one elderly gentleman seated outside on the pavement, nursing a tiny cup of double-strength coffee.

When ordering, you will need the Greek following phrases:

a Greek coffee	*éna ellinikó kafé*
no sugar	*skétos*
with milk	*me ghala*
medium sweet	*métrios*
strong and sweet	*varís ghlikós*

Even if you don't normally take sugar, try the medium-sweet version to get used to this way of drinking coffee.

And now it's your turn

The criteria for the preceding selection of tavernas and restaurants are that they are well established (in other words they've been around for a few years); produce consistently good food which is made on the premises; and have a menu that offers something more than just the standard dishes.

And you will probably be thinking: But Agnandio in Spartilas isn't mentioned! What about Dimitris? Why aren't there any tavernas mentioned in Kavos? (Mostly because there aren't any decent ones. If you have gone to Kavos, you are probably more interested in partying than what you are eating).

Which is why The Taste of a Place has a website – **www.the-taste-of-a-place.com** – where you can download information about recommended tavernas, or nominate your own favourites for inclusion. Look for the 'featured taverna' section: if a taverna has been recommended often enough by visitors to the site, it will be given a full write-up here. For details of how to nominate your favourite taverna see page 82.

Foraging for food

What to eat and drink – and where to find it

Shopping in Corfu

However you feel about getting the groceries back home, shopping for food on holiday can be a delight. Of course it can be a monumental drag as well, but on the whole Corfu provides plenty of opportunity for the fun of ferreting out the fresh and the unusual.

Resort supermarkets stay open all day and don't close until late, but it's more of an adventure to frequent smaller shops such as butchers. Just remember that these will close for the afternoon at 1pm, opening again around 5.30pm (punctuality not being of the essence). So grab your phrase book and go forth!

Supermarkets

Along the coast of Corfu, supermarkets are about as ubiquitous as souvenir shops. There are several big chains on the island, such as Dimitra, along with a plethora of independently owned 'mini-markets', so these days one can get most things most of the time. Mostly you will be nipping to the most convenient store in your area. But, if you plan to go shopping in Corfu Town, there are two supermarkets worth mentioning. Both are located on the main road into town from Paleokastrista.

Diellas (at the Danilia / Temploni junction) calls itself a discount centre; its stock is mostly, but not exclusively, Italian. So not only can you get tzakziki by the bucketful, you can also stock up on pancetta and parmesan. Other delights include Italian and Greek olive oil in five-litre cans, and speck (a type of German bacon) by the half-kilo block. The fruit and vegetable section also carries a wider range of produce than you'll find in most other supermarkets.

AB Vassilópoulos (on the left, 2km after the New Port / airport junction) does better than most for range and quality of meat, dairy and delicatessen. For example, its cheese counter offers 10 different types of feta; the deep-freeze cabinets contain surprises such as quail and pheasant; and, unusually, it has an organic corner (if you have ever watched the helicopters aerial-spraying pesticides over the olive groves, you will know that organically produced food has yet to become fashionable in Greece). Last but not least, AB staff are friendlier and more helpful than a lot of other supermarkets.

Butchers

You won't find butcher shops in resorts that grew up around villages too small to have them in the first place. But large inland villages such as Karrousades, Aghios Mattheos and Argirades all have at least one butcher, and there are also several in the centre of Corfu Town. When you do come across one, decide what you want before going in: the meat is rarely on display during the summer months (it is kept in a walk-in chill cabinet in the shop) and dithering isn't always advisable when you don't speak the language. Unless of course you want to spend a good 20 minutes playing charades, in which case remember that Greek chickens don't cock-a-doodle-do, they kik-kirri-coo, while waggling your behind in a playful manner to denote lambikins could get you into all sorts of trouble.

Meat tends to be stored as a whole or half animal, which the butcher cuts to order. Thus mince is beef-steak ground whilst you wait and watch. Lamb and kid are very similar in flavour and both are readily available. (What's the difference? With kid, the tails point up, with lamb, they point down.) Corfiot chickens are also very flavourful.

Fish

There are a variety of ways to buy fish on the island. First, if you are staying near a resort with a harbour, nip down to the quay first thing in the morning to see what the boats have bought in. In peak season most of the catch will have been already reserved for the restaurant trade, but in May or October you should have more luck.

You can also go fish-shopping at the stalls in Corfu Town's fruit and veg market (see page 16) or the shops in Vasiliou Street in the town centre. Outside Corfu Town there are only three or four fishmongers; the most helpful is in Acharavi in north Corfu. It is a father-and-son operation; the son, Nic Komaris, not only speaks English but, should you be feeling a bit out of your depth in the Mediterranean seafood scene, is happy to explain the difference between whitebait and sardines.

Finally, most Corfiot men list fishing as a hobby, so you may have the good fortune to be invited along on a fishing trip. This very early-morning adventure should carry a

health warning: do not try it if you have a hangover (choppy water will make it worse) and, if nets are involved, be prepared to come across the occasional fish that has been predated by huge, bright red and bristly wormy things. These ferocious creatures look like they'd view a big toe as an OK breakfast; rest assured, fish innards are their speciality. Even so, it is not pleasant coming across the realities of nature on an empty or bilious stomach.

However you acquire your fish, do not expect it to be cleaned and gutted for you. For your fishmonger to oblige a) you will have to be a regular customer and b) it will have to be a quiet moment in the day for him to spend the time away from his counter or catch. If he won't, turn to page 32 for tips on how to clean your own fish.

Bakeries

Greeks buy bread on a daily basis, so bakeries are everywhere, though there are now only five left in the whole of Corfu that use traditional, wood-burning ovens (all in and around Corfu Town and Benitses). For details of the kinds of bread available, turn to page 20.

On wheels

If you are staying in a rural location, don't forget to listen out for a truck with a blaring loudspeaker declaring something that, even if you understood Greek, would be unintelligible. This is not political canvassing, but a way of selling everything from carpets to live chickens and fresh fish. They tend to do the rounds at either end of the day (ie not siesta time). In addition to basics such as potatoes (the screech of *'patátes, patátes, patátes'* is sometimes discernable) the veggie van is a good place to find hórta – wild greens – when it's in season.

Are you being served?

Don't be put off by the off-hand behaviour of supermarket check-out staff – it is part of the job description and a consequence of having several hundred tourists a day produce a Dr10,000 note to pay for Dr1,000-worth of shopping when their purse is already bulging with change. The introduction of the euro could improve matters.

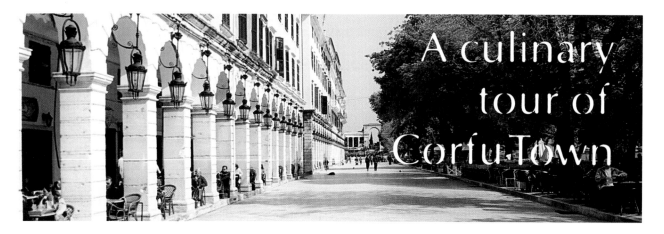

A culinary tour of Corfu Town

Museums, fortresses and churches are wonderful places to learn more about the history of a country. You'll find all of these in Corfu Town, but you can find out far more about everyday life and culture by doing what the Corfiots do in their spare time: socialising and shopping. And Corfu Town has to be one of the most attractive places in Greece to do this. Most visitors will hardly notice that behind the tourist shops, life continues. Down every side street and alleyway are tiny grocers and vegetable stalls that see steady custom the year round. So follow this culinary tour of the town and get a taste of what it is like to live here.

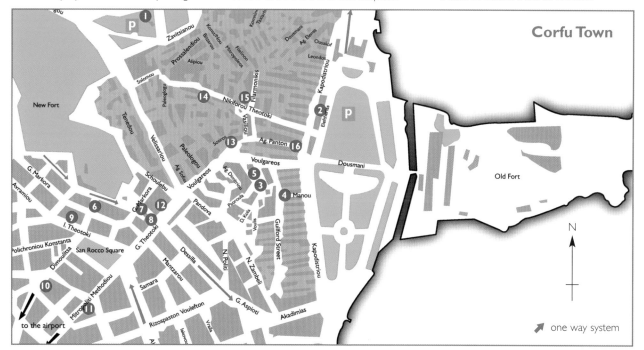

Parking

Be warned that traffic can be trying and it will be a major test of family harmony finding somewhere to park. There are two main car parks in the centre of town: by the **Old Port (1)** and in front of **The Liston (2)**. If you are confident of left-hand-drive cars with poor turning circles, and are unfazed by endless streams of scooters whose riders are infuriated by any show of hesitancy, then try your luck with roadside parking. But wherever you find a space remember you will need to buy a parking ticket. Car parks are pay as you enter; roadside parking

means finding a ticket warden, who will either be patrolling his patch or be stationed in what looks like a newspaper booth.

The faint of heart, or those wanting to buy fruit and vegetables, should aim to be parking in front of The Liston by 8.30am. Any later than this and you will find yourself queueing for a space. Outside of peak season, it won't be too much of a problem, but in August expect a sneak preview of hell: heat, horses, and hordes of people as lost as you are. And you will get lost. The one-way system in Corfu Town went through a phase of changing almost weekly in the run up to the EU summit that was held here in 1994, and most road maps are still inaccurate.

At this point you will probably need a coffee to recover, if only from the trauma of having got out of bed so early. The most civilised place is the **Town Hall Square (3)** at the bottom of Guilford Street, where three establishments offer coffee and fresh orange juice. From here you can plan the order of your morning.

Town Hall Square

First on the list should be a visit to two shops in Town Hall Square, starting with **Starenio (4)**, at 52 Guilford Street. Nicholas and Anna Kondopolous aren't sure how to describe their delightful, if tiny, shop. They sell bread – sourced from the three bakeries in town that still have wood-fired ovens – but Starenio is not a bakery. Their cakes, made in the kitchen out back, range from stewed-plum-covered sponges to moist honey-and-nut cakes, but the couple are keen to point out that they are very different from a '*zacharoplasteion*' – the Greek equivalent of a patisserie. And they are particularly proud of their homemade jams and marmalades – fig marmalade is one of the most popular of the range.

They choose ingredients for their quality – the sausage in the pasta pie, for example, is sourced from an artisan salami maker in Corfu who makes them in very limited quantities. Anna makes a range of other open-topped pies using her own filo pastry. These vary according to what is in season, but may include leek, spinach, or chicken – which you can buy by the slice. And for those of you who don't want to 'take away' there are four tiny tables on the pavement outside the shop for customers. At lunchtime, Starenio offers a no-choice, savoury dish to eat. The decision about what this is going to be each day is taken in the morning and, according to Nicholas, 'depends on the mood and intuition of the cook'; it might be pork in lemon sauce or *dolmades* made with cabbage leaves. Don't forget to try their cookies and savoury nibbles, such as golfball-sized *spanokopitta* – spinach and cheese pies – that are just the thing to accompany a sun-downer gin and tonic.

To experience a *zacharoplasteion* (which literally means 'sugar-sculptor') walk across the Town Hall Square to **Patisserie Kritikos (5)**. This is an absolute must for the sweet-toothed: crème cakes, pastries, tarts and chocolates galore are all made on the premises. A particular favourite are the chocolate-covered slithers of candied orange peel or kumquats.

New Fort Market

If you want to visit the **fish, fruit and veg market (6)** alongside the New Fort, go there before it closes down for the day at around 1pm. There are a couple things to bear in mind. Firstly it is not a tourist attraction – it is full of people trying to get their shopping done before the kids get home from school. (Imagine if there were a bunch of tourists blocking the veggie aisle at your local supermarket back home, exclaiming 'good Lord, they sell parsnips!') Stallholders are thus in as much of a rush as their customers. Ninety-nine per cent of them are a jolly bunch who are keen to help; still, very occasionally you will come across someone bad-tempered who will try to charge you for a kilo's worth of beetroot when the scales say the weight is rather a lot less. So keep your wits about you. Remember, too, to go with plenty of small change and, although a lot of the vendors speak some English (especially the younger ones), you will elicit more smiles if you attempt some Greek. Key phrases include:

Half a kilo	Miso kilo
One kilo	Ena kilo
100 grams	Ekató gram
How much?	Póso káni?
Please	Parakahló
Thank you	Efahristó

The fish stalls are concentrated at the bottom end of the market. The men behind the counter are usually fishermen, come straight off their boats after a night's work.

If you decide you want a couple of steaks from a large fish, such as bonito, the fishmonger may appear to ignore you. Do not be put off, because all he is doing is waiting until there are sufficient buyers to make it worth everyone's while to cut it up.

Crowded around the fish stalls and spilling onto the road are invariably a collection of Greek farmers and peasants, perched on upturned crates selling what surplus they have from their allotments and farms. These farmers are generally well worth checking

out; they could be selling anything, from spring onions to punnets of mulberries or cherries. In spring, there is a brief, wonderful, spell when wild strawberries make an appearance, carefully cushioned in vine leaves.

Further on, fish and farmers give way to the permanent vegetable stalls. The great joy of buying here is the freshness of the produce. Fruit has its bloom, courgettes still have bees investigating their flower blossoms and tomatoes smell like they have spent time growing in proper sunlight. But prices vary according the quality of the produce, so don't stop at the first mound of luscious-looking plums – walk the length of the market before making any purchases.

Besides veggies, look out for honey: the local stuff is wonderfully aromatic, which isn't really surprising considering the bees have foraged across hills and fields full of herbs such as thyme and *rigani* (see page 38). Stalls selling olives are concentrated in the middle part of the market (try before you buy, as some of the local olives can have an intense flavour), and in autumn, you can find fig cakes called *sykópitta* (see page 20) for sale. These are a Corfiot speciality, go very well with cheese, and make excellent presents for foodie friends.

Desilla Street to San Rocco Square

Next pay a visit to the **cheese shop (7)** on Desilla Street, on the left 20m down the road from the market. The selection of cheeses isn't huge but what they have is good quality: they actually taste of something, not plastic or soap. Bear in mind the feta is hidden in a tin behind the counter.

If you want to experience lunch in a real Greek taverna that caters for office workers

and stallholders, try **Rouvas (8)** at 13 Desilla Street. The kitchen is open to the dining area, whose walls are covered with aged posters of Greece, and helpings are hearty and cheap. Dishes include stuffed tomatoes, green bean stew and *stifado*. Eat well, for you are about to embark on a booze-cruise about town and you have a choice of several venues, depending on your budget and enthusiasm. The main thing to remember is to arm yourself with several empty water bottles first.

From the restaurant you can nip round the corner via San Rocco Square to **Cava Vaeni (9)** on the right hand side of I Theotoki – it isn't numbered but is next door to a Kodak shop. It stocks a reasonable selection of wine (the top end of their range includes Amethystos) but the real reason for visiting here is to fill some of your empty water bottles with retsina from the in-store barrel.

Head back up the road to San Rocco square and take a road called Dimoulitsa on the right, which goes out of town towards the airport. You don't need to go that far. Walk for five minutes and you will see the

mental hospital on your right. Opposite is an old-fashioned taverna called **Cava Castellano (10)** that sells nothing but wine by the barrel. This is a family-run business; the daughter, who trained as a chemist, now makes the wine. There is a choice of red and white, and you can even blend your own, spending a happy hour perfecting a rosé to suit your palate. Restaurant owners buy wine here to sell by the carafe, and Greek friends swear you can drink masses of it and never get a hangover.

Alternatively, head for **Musses (11)**, a national chain of wine shops that also sell a wide range of nuts and *glykos* (sweets). This is just off San Rocco Square on the left hand side of Mitropoliti Methodiou road.

Back onto Voulgareos Street

Budget wine quota satisfied, your next stop could be to the car to deposit all those bottles; but if your shopping bag still has room, the next shop is **Coffeeway (12)** at 9 Voulgareos Street. If you are not a fan of instant or Greek coffee, you may be one of those poor souls who fill half their suitcase with packets of Kenyan 'AA' arabica

coffee to take on holiday. Now, thanks to Coffeeway, you can travel hand-luggage-only to Corfu. It has a wide range of products: whole coffee beans ground to order, teas, and implements ranging from cafetieres to Turkish coffee pots.

Vasiliou Street

There used to be several dairy shops dotted about Corfu Town, but with the advent of supermarkets, they changed into fast-food joints or clothes boutiques. The **dairy shop (13)** at 10 Vasiliou Street is easy to miss because it is nothing more than a walk-in refrigerator. There is a lone wooden chair on which you wait to be served by the woman behind the huge chill cabinet. This contains unmarked plastic tubs brimming with a choice of rice pudding (heaven with a dusting of cinnamon), plain custard, chocolate custard and yoghurts. On top sits a huge block of cows' milk butter — tempting but not an option unless you have a chill bag with you. If you do have one, there are several butchers' shops on the right as you wander down Vasiliou Street to help you stock up for that barbeque you have been planning.

Nikiforou Theotoki Street

Now devote yourself to some serious shopping. Vasiliou Street runs into Nikiforou Theotoki Street. Turn left and 50m further down the road is **Kostas Thymis (14)**, a cave under the arches at 74 Nikiforou Theotoki, which stocks a good selection of the quality Greek wines. Posh wine means non-anglicised labels, but you don't need to know the difference between Assyrtiko and Aghiorghitiko (indigenous Greek grape varieties) since the owner is charming and, even though he doesn't speak English, is of a generation that is chivalrous, polite and delighted if you are interested in wine. So go with the intention of buying a bottle or three.

Kyrie Thymis' stock includes:

Amethystos	Red, white and rosé
Gentilini Robola	A lovely lemony, honey-tasting wine from Cephalonia
Gerovassiliou	Red and white – the latter is regarded as a real trendsetter on the Greek wine scene
Ktima Arghyrou Santorini	An intense, mouth-wateringly good wine

Filarmonikis Street to Kapodistriou Street

As you walk towards The Liston from the wine shop, Filarmonikis Street will be on your left. And if any of your party are now close to mutiny, now is the time to bribe good behaviour with the promise of *loukoumathes*. These are doughnuts with no hole in the middle, served dusted with cinnamon and sugar. Needless to say they

are completely delicious – especially since they come straight from a bubbling cauldron of hot oil. Find them at the **doughnut shop (15)**, three doors down on the left-hand side of Filarmonikis Street. It is tiny – they serve customers through a window counter. And if doughnuts aren't your thing, try the **Haägen Dazs ice cream parlour (16)**, behind The Liston on the corner of Kapodistriou and Ag. Panton Street.

Finish at The Liston

Stagger down the road with your purchases to **The Liston (2)** and gratefully park yourself outside one of the bars that line it; perhaps an *ouzeri* called Zisomos at the palace end of the arcade that is a favourite with locals. Whatever liquid refreshment you chose, remember to ask for some *mezethes* to nibble whilst you enjoy people-watching. If you want to show off, say something like 'let's have a *pikilia* later'; you of course will know that *pikilia* refers to a more elaborate collection of savoury dishes, while *mezethes* are something simple like a plate of olives or salami.

Storecupboard staples

There are some ingredients that, even if you are determined to do no cooking whatsoever on holiday, you will still end up buying.

Bread

(Psomí / ψωμί)

Bread isn't just served up to tourists to keep them happy while they wait for their order, it is an integral part of a Greek meal. Corfu is no exception. As recently as 20 years ago, farmers were still growing their own wheat on the terracing underneath Mount Pantecrator. If you spend a day exploring this area, look out for the old, round threshing floors. These were carefully positioned so that the wind that whistles up the valleys would blow the chaff away. Bread is bought on a daily basis and sells out very quickly, so get to the baker before 10am if you want a choice. Some of the breads you might see include:

Simicto: soft-crusted bread, which lasts better than the crunchy-crust type

Franjola: two loaves joined down the middle – you do not have to buy both; if you want want just one, ask for '*mea franjola*'

Kouloura: literally means round, but the loaf also has a hole in the middle

Karveli: a round loaf with no hole

Mavro: the Greek word for black, but if you ask for '*mavro psomí*', you will be given a wholemeal loaf

Coffee

(Kafé / καφές)

In terms of what you can buy at the supermarket, there is a fairly wide choice. Bear in mind that in the same way Sellotape is used as a generic word for sticky tape, so Nescafe is the brand everyone refers to in Greece when it comes to instant coffee. Alas, if you can distinguish between Arabica and Robusta, or the difference a roast can make to a coffee bean, you will have to slum it – or bring your favoured blend with you.

Greek coffee, using beans that have been ground into almost a powder, is heart-stoppingly strong and takes stamina to get used to. The best place to experience Greek coffee is in a *kafeneion* (see page 11).

Fig cake

(Sykópitta / συκοπιτα)

Not strictly a basic, but really a worthwhile purchase. Wrapped in vine leaves and tied with string, these delicacies are the size and shape of Camembert – and there the similarity ends. For instead of cheese, inside you'll find a compressed mixture of minced, dried green fig, grape must, pepper and ouzo. Recipes vary, but the result is a solid, sweet, tangy patty that is particularly aromatic if bay leaves have been interspersed with the vine-leaf wrapping. It sounds dubious – but they are delicious. Traditionally, *sykópittes* are served along with brandy at the end of a meal. Look for them in the fruit and vegetable markets in September and October.

Honey

(Méli / μέλι)

Two factors influence the taste of honey. The first is the flowers the bees have been gathering nectar from. Corfiot honey tastes great because the absence of large-scale cereal farming makes for an abundance of wildflowers. Secondly, honey that you have had to trudge along to the local hive owner for, empty jam jar in hand, is somehow much more delicious than that bunged at the last minute into the supermarket trolley. Like the bee, you will have to work for it. But once you have made it your mission to buy some local honey you will start noticing bee hives everywhere and, off the main coastal road, you can sometimes spot signs of honey for sale. The fruit and vegetable market in Corfu Town is also a good place to buy it.

Olive oil

(Eleólatho / ελαόλαδο)

Although large areas of Corfu are covered with olive trees, and the oil produced is golden and very pleasant, it is not considered the best that Greece has to offer.

This is due to the way the olives are picked,

or rather not picked: the fruit is left to fall into nets. (Some Greeks – including Corfiots – complain this is laziness, but whether or not this is the case, the large, spreading nature of the trees make it very difficult to pick the olives or to knock them out with a pole.) Fallen fruit can bruise or be over-ripe and this in turn affects the quality of the oil by increasing the acidity. The term is a bit confusing: 'acidity' doesn't refer to the sharpness of lemons or vinegar, but instead to the amount of free fatty acids present in the oil. It is a way of measuring the degree of oxidation of the oil, which increases quite quickly in hot conditions. The best extra-virgin olive oil has a very low acidity – less than one per cent – and is made from under-ripe olives, picked from the tree, which are processed as soon as possible after harvesting. Above 3.3 per cent acidity and the stuff is only fit for lubricating engines.

In Corfu, the olive season lasts from November to well into spring, and farmers will check their nets on a daily basis – in theory anyway. Oil and olives change in look and flavour as the harvest season progresses. Oil from the most common variety of Corfiot olive is orange at the start

of the season. The 'Koroneikes' variety, in contrast, produces greenish oil to begin with, similar to the peppery Italian 'super' oils. Later in the season, once the olives have ripened properly, the oil from both varieties is golden and mellower in flavour.

It is, however, not that easy to find good Corfiot olive oil. A combination of EU agricultural policy, the more lucrative profits from tourism and (at the time of writing) some adverse weather conditions during the flowering seasons over the last couple of years, combine to make it quite difficult to come by.

One really needs a Greek friend to effect an introduction with a local olive press while they are active (up until Easter-time). If you are lucky enough, then take a freshly baked loaf along with you: rub a cut clove of garlic over the bread, drizzle with oil, sprinkle with salt and pepper (don't worry – someone will have the ingredients), and you have the perfect mid-morning snack.

And if you aren't that lucky? Choose one of the two good brands of extra-virgin olive oil that are widely available in the shops: Iliada and Karyatis.

Preserve your own olives

Olives cannot be picked and eaten straight from the tree. So in the serendipitous event that you are given some fresh olives, here is how you turn them from being inedible to delicious:

Slit the side of each olive with a sharp knife. Immerse the olives in cold water and change this water every day for 10 days or longer – taste the water to see if all the bitterness has disappeared. After this, the olives should spend three to four weeks in a very strong brine solution. Legend has it the right salinity has been reached when a raw egg will float in it, but a more scientific way of going about things is to mix a generous 150g of pure sodium chloride with each litre of water (don't use table salt, as its anti-caking agents will lower the salinity).

The olives, stored in an airtight container in a cool, dark place, will then be ready to eat. If you prefer a vinegar tang, rinse them and serve mixed with equal quantities of olive oil and vinegar, plus seasonings such as garlic or the herb *rigani* (see page 38).

Olives
(Eliés / ελιές)

The most delicious and well-known of Greek olives is the Kalamata – grown in the region of the same name on the Peleponnese part of the mainland. This olive is widely available on Corfu preserved in brine or oil, whether with or without spices and garlic. Confusingly, you may come across bottled olive oil labelled 'Kalamata extra-virgin olive oil'. This is actually made from the Koroneikes olive, grown in the Kalamata region.

Generally in Greece, the olives one makes olive oil from aren't the same varieties as those that one eats. Corfu is an exception, because farmers didn't have much choice about the type of olive they planted during the period of Venetian rule. Thus the black Lianolia olive is the most commonly planted variety and it is used for both oil production and pickling.

The Lianolia olive is much smaller than the Kalamata. Its stone has a sharp point and, although usually marinated with herbs, it can sometimes taste bitter. A local favourite is another variety described as the 'fat' olive. This is because the fruit is round in shape and has a dimple in the end opposite to where the stalk was.

The best place to buy olives is the fruit and veg market in Corfu Town. Appearance and price give an idea of quality – you get what you pay for – but it is worth asking for an olive to try before buying some.

Pasta
(Zymariká / ζυμαρικά)

The Greek word *pásta* refers to gateaux-type sweets served alongside your coffee in the kafeneion. *Zymariká* is the Greek word for pasta in general; *makaroní*, thank goodness, means macaroni.

Pulses
(Óspria / όσπρια)

Dried beans come in all shapes and sizes; the most common on taverna menus are gigantes, or butter beans cooked in a tomato sauce (so popular perhaps because they can be bought in catering-size tins). You can buy beans either in packets or by the shovelful in all the supermarkets and markets – and digging for your beans out of the sack is just so much more fun!

You may come across the term '*fava*' – in the United States this means a broad bean, but in Greece it refers to yellow split peas, which are boiled until soft and then pureed with olive oil and seasoned to make a dip.

Fasolia, a hugely popular dish all over Greece, is usually made with haricot beans. There are as many variations on this recipe as there are cooks, but the one thing Greeks agree on is the importance of using rainwater – water from the tap tends to be full of chemicals and calcium that makes it 'hard'. And hard water turns bean skins tough and stops them from cooking to a nice, even, floury texture.

This leaves the enthusiastic cook with a problem. Splashing out on bottled water to boil beans in is, well, mad. But the days of rain-filled water cisterns are gone, because most houses, thank goodness, are now connected to mains water. So Greek advice is: put a pinch of baking soda into the boiling water at the start of cooking and don't add any salt until just before the end.

Furthermore, I am assured by an animal nutritionist – who understands the reaction of beans in the intestines – that to minimise flatulence (my apologies to readers of a delicate disposition), you should soak the beans for 24 hours and then boil them really hard rfor 15 minutes at the beginning of the cooking time.

If boiling dried pulses requires too much in the way of advance planning, check the freezer cabinets of your local supermarket for frozen 'white beans'. (The picture on the packet is of white beans flecked with red.) You only need to simmer these for 20 minutes, and the result is much tastier than tinned beans.

Having said that, there is nothing like having a tin of beans in the cupboard when all you want to do in the way of cooking is find an tin-opener. There are several Greek brands commonly available, with only slight differences in recipes. Look for small flat tins of butter or haricot beans 'cooked in tomato and spices'. They are quite nice, as long as you don't take a spoonful expecting Heinz. Your taste buds will have an identity crisis as the sauce contains, among other herbs, dill.

Rice
(Rísi / ρύζι)

If you are happy with American rice, then you will be spoilt for choice. But if you are after rice suitable for risotto or a pilaf, then you will need to spend a couple of minutes scrutinising the packet. For example, Agrino is a common brand that sells about seven different varieties of rice. 'ΦΙΝΟ' – or *fino* – is okay for pilaffs and stuffing vegetables; whilst 'ΛΑΙΣ' will do for risotto. Varieties such as Arborio or Basmati are more difficult to come by.

Tea
(Tsái / τσάι)

Twinings, PG Tips, tea bags, herbal, floral, prickly stems, decaffeinated … you name it, a supermarket somewhere will have it.

Vinegar
(Ksythi / ξύδι)

Don't bother with imported varieties, as Greek vinegar is much nicer and cheaper. It is sold in little plastic bottles and is a light red-brown colour. Its flavour is sprightly, without being industrial-strength. In rural areas, people still make their own, but you are unlikely to find this homemade vinegar for sale.

Fridge essentials

Even basic holiday homes will have a small fridge, so make use of it to store both everyday and more exotic foods.

Anchovies in oil

(Antsóies sto láthi / αντζούγιες στο λάδι)

Don't buy the tiny tins of anchovy fillets; you'll only end up with a semi-open, broken lid, a lacerated forefinger and smelly oil all over the place. Head for the deli counter and buy them by weight instead. True, you will be given a bag full of fillets that may well leak oil, but the risk is worth it, as the contents will be far superior.

One tip. When using anchovies in a sauce, try mashing them in with the oil or other ingredients before frying the mixture: anchovy fried on its own can taste bitter.

Butter

(Voútiro / βούτυρο)

Cooking savoury dishes with butter is unusual in most of Greece; instead Greeks use it for making pastries. But where the peppery taste of olive oil is unsuitable, they prefer clarified butter – you will find it stocked alongside the ordinary kind.

If you are feeling adventurous, check out sheep butter, identifiable by its sheep-head graphic on silver foil paper. Try it thickly spread on a slice of still-warm bread and enjoy the subtly different flavour.

Foodie zealots may be interested in tracking down the best sheep's butter, which comes from an area called Zagoria on the mainland – about a two-hour drive from Igoumenitsa, the mainland port just across from Corfu. In early spring, when the sheep have been grazing on new grass, it is worth going on a weekend pilgrimage to a mountain village to experience the utterly ambrosial combination of mountain honey, sheep's butter and bread from a wood-fired oven.

Cheese

(Tiri / τυρί)

Corfu no longer produces cheese commercially and even if its dairy industry were still thriving, it certainly couldn't cope with the influx of tourists. So a lot of dairy produce comes from a large cooperative near Ioaninna on the mainland. But it's easy enough to find Greek, if not Corfiot, cheese at a deli counter or, better still, a dedicated cheese shop.

Commonly available cheeses fall into roughly three categories:

Greek hard cheeses	graveria, kaseri, képhalotyri, metsovoni
Greek soft cheeses	feta, kopanistí, manouri, myzithra
Imported cheeses	gouda, edam, parmesan, masdama

Guidebooks often suggest that *képhalotyri* is the Greek equivalent of parmesan, but a closer approximation is a hard pecorino. It doesn't have the nutty, rounded flavour of parmesan; the comparison is probably more to do with the fact that cooks use it in much the same way.

Kaseri is, to be honest, rather an uninteresting cheese. The Greeks call it 'factory cheese' because it is reconstituted from the curds of *képhalotyri*.

A good *graviera* is delicious – it is the Greek equivalent of gruyere. Most regions of Greece produce a *graviera* and they are all slightly different in flavour, so ask for a small bit to try before choosing.

To make a good *saganaki* (fried cheese), use the smoked cheese called *metsovoni kapnisto*.

It has a firm, slightly rubbery texture, comes from the Epirius region on the mainland, and is made from either cow's or sheep's milk.

Feta needs no explaining. But as easy as it is to produce and buy, quality varies. The very best feta is aged in oak barrels, and is made mainly in the Peloponnese and parts of the Epirus. And you will need to visit those areas to find it. Easier to come by in Corfu is feta that has been aged in large tins – this in turn is better than plastic-wrapped cheese. If it is too salty, soak it in water for a few hours – it will come to no harm and taste better for it.

Kopanistí is a blue goats cheese – only it isn't blue, green or grey to look at, rather a flesh-tinted white. I suspect the stuff is addictive: with the first nibble, your reaction will be 'weird', then you'll think 'well I didn't quite understand the taste, let me try it again' and an hour later significant inroads have been made into the cheese in the name of scientific research.

Mizíthra should be mentioned if only because of the reaction it produces in Greeks: eyes light up or roll heavenwards depending on whether you ask if they know of it or where one can find it. It is similar to ricotta in texture and flavour and, ideally, made from sheep's milk.

The only time the fresh unsalted cheese is likely to make an appearance in the shops is spring. But salted *mizíthra* is quite often available; some people compare it to cottage cheese on the basis that both cheeses have a low fat content. In fact, the texture is different – cottage cheese is more clotted and lumpy – and *mizíthra* is more salty. There is one other version of this cheese, one that is left to dry and harden before being used for grating.

Make your own mizíthra

If you want to know why the Greeks make such a fuss about this delicious curd cheese, try making it yourself. First find a lactating ewe. To make around 200g of cheese you will need to extract two litres of milk from her. Hot-foot it off the hillside to the nearest available kitchen. Heat the milk in a stainless steel saucepan and as soon as it starts to boil, remove from the heat and add the juice of a lemon (without pips, naturally). Stir until it curdles i.e. it starts to look like soured milk. If the milk does not oblige, return it to a gentle heat until it does. Then pour very slowly through a sieve that has been lined with two layers of muslin.

The stuff that is left in the sieve is called curds and the liquid that you have either poured down the sink or kept in a bowl is called the whey. (In remote parts of the world, such as Turkmenistan, drinking the whey with your favoured tipple is believed to help prevent hangovers. Try it. You'll feel green round the gills long before you are over the limit.)

Fold the muslin over the curds and place a weighted plate on top to squeeze out more of the whey. Ideally pop it in the fridge overnight; the resulting curd cheese should be eaten within two to three days.

Filo pastry

(Phyllo / Φύλλο πίττας)

Pitta means pie in Greek, the most famous *pitta* of them all being *tyropitta* – cheese pie – which is made with filo pastry. However, in Corfu not all *pittes* are made with filo, particularly savoury ones. Occasionally a cook will make a thicker, homemade version of filo for an open-topped *pitta* (a kind of quiche, in other words) because commercial filo pastry is too fine to support the pie's contents.

Filo is, of course, widely available and the trick to using it successfully is to let it come to room temperature without letting it dry out. If the pastry is cold or dry it will crack and tear.

Ice-cream

(Pagotó / παγωτό)

Parents will have daily difficulty getting their children past the 'Algida' ice-cream cabinet stationed outside every supermarket – Algida is virtually identical to the Wall's brands available in northern Europe. As for Greek brands, there are several. For example, Delta doesn't only do diary products and fruit juices; 'Nirvana' – which comes in tubs – is one of its popular ice-creams aimed more at grown-ups.

The health-conscious should look for tiny yoghurt pots with sticks in the chill cabinets. The idea is that once you have got them home, you put the sticks into the pots and then into the freezer. Hey presto! Yoghurt lollipops.

If you are in north-east Corfu and have a hankering for Italian ice-cream, then check out Ice-Dream at the Perithia turn-off (diagonally opposite an Eko petrol station) on the road that runs between Kassiopi and Acharavi. This gelataria makes its ice-creams on the premises using proper milk and cream, with no preservatives. Fruit is fresh and the other ingredients – such as the hazelnut syrup – are brought over from Italy. The owner, trained in Italy, claims to be the only artisanal ice-cream maker like this in Corfu, and supplies several of the restaurants in the area.

Milk

(Ghála / γάλα)

Twenty years ago fresh milk was impossible to find, except direct from the cow. These days the difficulties are whether Light means Diet and does 1.5 per cent fat equate to semi-skimmed (no and yes respectively). The local Corfiot brand is Farmer or **Φαρμα**, which also makes delicious rice pudding.

Pickled vegetables

(Toursía / τουρσία)

A favourite nibble all over Greece, *toursía* are small, mild chilli peppers stuffed with slithers of cucumber or cabbage stalk. Find them at the deli counter.

Salted mullet roe

(Taramás / ταραμάς)

The main ingredient (well, it should be) in a taramosalata. It comes in two forms: pink and grey. The former is dyed; the latter is not – and guess which one is better. Salted mullet roe is one of Europe's oldest edible luxuries: the Greeks first started importing it from the Ancient Egyptians and the *salata* came about as a way of making this delicacy go further. They then started making it themselves but grey mullet are now scarce in the Mediterranean, so these days the Greeks import cod's roe from countries such as Norway. You may not want to

bother making the *salata*, since it requires
a large pestle and mortar – for purists with
time on their hands – or a food processor
(see page 53 for our recipe). But *taramás*
freezes well, so it is worth taking back home
where it is much more difficult to come by.
While in Corfu, ask for it at the deli counter.

Yoghurt

(Ghiaoúti / γιαούρτι)

Most people have come across Greek
yoghurt. These days it comes in an array of
disguises: half-fat, no-fat, flavoured or not.
Furthermore, if you don't fancy Greek, you
can opt for the German and French brands
that are also readily available. But since the
difference between half-fat and full-fat
yoghurt is a couple of peanuts per 100ml
and if, like most holidaymakers, you'll be
blowing your daily recommended calorific
intake on alcohol alone, how about going for
the real McCoy and loving every mouthful?

At all supermarket deli counters, hidden in
large buckets, will be plain, strained, whole
milk yoghurt. Purchase with some honey, stir
the two together according to taste, and
demolish with a teaspoon, very slowly, with
the Ionian Sea in the distance. Heaven.

Meat

The quality of meat available is high in Corfu, although the cuts or joints may be somewhat different from those you are used to back home.

Beef

(Moshári / μοσχάρι)

The Greek habit of butchers preparing a cut to order is commendable, because there is no chance of being given unwanted bits of the animal in disguise, as is the case with supermarket 'mince'. At the butchers, mince (*kimás* in Greek) is ground beefsteak, pure and simple.

Quite often, the term 'veal' appears on a taverna menu. This actually means beef from a yearling animal that has been milk-weaned, so there is no need to worry about how it was reared.

Chicken

(Kotópoulo / κοτόπουλο)

A chicken is pretty much recognisable as chicken all over the planet; but here in Corfu they still manage to taste of something. Lorries go round the villages every week selling live ones, for egg-laying or for the pot which might account for their lovely full flavour.

Lamb

(Arní / αρνί)

Lamb is the meat eaten to celebrate Easter Sunday – Easter being a far more important occasion in Greece than Christmas. Lamb offal is also tremendously popular. At this time of year grillrooms serve *kokorétsi*, or spit-roasted offal. Another way of serving lamb offal is *maghirítsa*, a stew or soup that sometimes has the famous Greek egg-and-lemon sauce called *avgolémono* (see page 74) stirred into it just before serving. Quite often, roast lamb will follow, while grilled or roast lamb shoulder, leg or chops are also available for those who don't feel quite so adventurous.

More unusually, a sausage called *horthi* may be made from the lamb's innards – this is grilled and then served as an appetiser.

Pork

(Hirinó / χοιρινό)

Souvlakia – skewered pieces of grilled meat – are usually made with pork unless specifically indicated otherwise. See page 72 for advice on how to cook your own.

Loukanika horiatika is the Corfiot term for country sausages. They should be very meaty and chunky, flavoured with pepper and herbs, with little or no rusk. They aren't that easy to find in supermarkets, but try asking for them at a butchers.

Nómboulo is smoked pork fillet and is a Corfiot speciality. Use in the same way you would an air-dried ham: slice thinly and serve as mezethes; or use to beef up a scrambled-egg sandwich or pasta salad. You are guaranteed to find it at the factory where it is produced, along with local salami and sausages. This is on the Paleocastritsa road out of Corfu Town, before the turning to Sidari. In between a Shell petrol station and a pottery on the right, you will notice a large white building with a small sign outside saying 'Corfu Agricultural Organic Greek Products'. Even though there is no indication of a shop, walk in and ask – the staff are happy to oblige.

Rabbit

(Kounéli / κουνέλι)

Traditionally, *stifado* – a red wine ragout with small whole onions – was made using rabbit. But there aren't any wild rabbits left in Corfu, so these days it is as likely to be made with a commercially reared rabbit or any other type of suitable meat.

Wild game

(Kenyee / κυνήγι)

During the winter months, Corfu turns into
a war zone, with the roads lined every
afternoon with men crouched behind their
cars, clutching shot guns and looking intently
at the sky. It sounds like a war zone too,
with the olive groves reverberating to the
sound of gunfire. Their quarry? Anything
feathered – thrushes, wood pigeons, robins.
For this, they need a gun dog (presumably
because the birds are so small that once
shot they are difficult to find). Hence nearly
every dog on the island is a Pointer or a
Pointer Allsorts.

Eating the birds isn't really the object of the
exercise – ask a hunter about how they are
cooked and they are vague (the birds are
given to their mothers, their wives no longer
having the time or the inclination to pluck
and gut the carcasses). Thus the pastime
these days is more about chaps taking time
out – and it is the one and only time of the
day when their mobiles are turned off. So
should you fancy pheasant or duck, buy
fresh birds during the season at better
supermarkets. Miles safer.

Fish

Fresh, locally caught fish tends to be expensive because there is not much of it around, especially in the summer months. So most of the fish that appears in tavernas, even if fresh, is likely to be imported. There is nothing wrong with this of course – just don't let someone con you about its origins. The following species are commonly available in the fish markets or on taverna menus.

For grilling
Mackerel

(Scoumbrí / σκουμρί)

Mackerel – up to 50cms long, with a dark-blue back and wavy, dark blue lines along its upper sides – are plentiful and available all year round in Corfu, yet for some inexplicable reason, they never feature on taverna menus. Change the situation by asking for it! It not only tastes good, it is also not endangered by over-fishing.

Sea bass

(Lavrákia / λαβράκια)

The deep-chested, white-bellied sea bass is very trendy and consequently wild stocks have fallen to dangerous levels, so you may be aware that some restaurants back home no longer serve it. But the good news is that it is farmed in Corfu – the sea cages are visible as one drives out of Kassiopi towards Acharavi. Apparently the fish are allowed to grow naturally, thus minimising the difference in quality between the locally farmed and wild sea bass.

Recipes for the fish stew *bianco* (see page 62) sometimes suggest using sea bass. But you might find that its flavour is too delicate for the large amounts of garlic, lemon and potato involved.

Swordfish

(Xiphios / ξιφίας)

Swordfish swim into Corfiot waters during the winter months in pursuit of small prey, but it doesn't often appear as a fresh, whole fish – you are more likely to find it as small chunks in kebabs, or frozen as ready-sliced steaks. The white, meaty flesh is extremely popular and in summer it has to be imported to satisfy demand.

Unfortunately, the species is in serious decline due to over-fishing: so if you have an environmental conscience, avoid it. Either stick to chicken, or be adventurous and try a different fish.

Red mullet

(Barbouni / μπαρμπούνι)

Red mullet are easy to spot in the market because of the two whiskers, or barbells, under their chins, plus, of course, the colour. Apparently you can tell if a red mullet has been caught off the coast of Corfu because it will be a rosier hue than imported specimens. It is bony to eat, but delicious. Picky eaters may find its boniness problematic, but on the other hand its flesh is delicious.

For frying
Anchovy

(Gávros / γάβρος)

Most of us think of anchovies as bony pink strips that emerge dripping in oil from the tin or the jar in which they have been packed. But fresh, they are silver all over, with a receding lower jaw, and a maximum size of 20cms. The flesh is soft and oily, but salting firms it up – hence the popularity of this method of preserving it.

Excellent deep-fried, or eaten 'marinata': simply fillet a spanking fresh fish and pickle it in lemon juice for a couple of days.

Picarel

(Maríthes / μαρίδες)

Picarel are silver all over, about 10cms long, with a dark blotch behind the gills, and if small are often sold under the name 'whitebait'. Other similar-looking small fish include *ghopa* (Latin name *Boops boops*) which aren't quite as tasty. Whichever, they all tend to get the whitebait treatment: lightly battered and deep-fried.

Sardines

(Sardélles / σαρδέλες)

Sardines are fished the whole year round in Corfu's coastal waters: the only time when they are not caught is during the full moon or when bad weather prevents it. They are very popular on the island – people sometimes stomp out of the shop empty-handed when they have discovered there are none for sale. Recognise them out of the tin by the two spots behind the gills.

For baking, grilling, or poaching

Bonito

(Palamítha / παλαμίδα)

Deep grey to deep blue on the back, with long slanting stripes on its sides, bonito are handsome creatures – a sort of Saab version of the mackerel, but with flesh that is not as dark or oily. Larger fish can be cut into steaks, rather like tuna.

Grey mullet

(Képhanoi / κέφαλος)

There are several species of grey mullet, but the one you'll find in Corfu is *Mugil cephalus*, which has a large flat head (hence its Greek name, which means 'head'). It is streamlined, silver all over, with a small mouth, and is usually sold when it is about 30cms long. The quality of the fish depends on where it has been feeding: the best are those that are caught out to sea. A good choice for those who like an easy eat, as it doesn't have lots of little bones lurking in the fillets.

Gilt-head bream

(Tsipoúra / τσιπούρα)

Lovely looking, with a white belly, dark grey back and a creamy yellow, crescent-shaped band between its eyes, bream tastes great and is also easy to manage from the bone point of view, whether in fillets or served whole. Bream hasn't been over-fished as much as other species and is also farmed (though not in Corfu), so you can enjoy it with an easy conscience.

Squid

(Kalamária / καλαμάρια)

Squid look like baggy condoms with frilly bits. They are either almost transparent or milky white, and can grow up to 50cms long – though most never get to be this size. The thing to remember about squid is that it should either be cooked briefly, or for ages – nothing in between, otherwise it will be tough. Frozen ones have the advantage of being ready prepared, but the texture may be rubbery.

(Incidentally, for those of you learning to speak Greek, *kalamári* – how it's often referred to when people first attempt the language – is actually the singular form of the noun. If you're buying or ordering more than one squid, use the plural: *kalamária*.)

Speciality fish

Eels

(Hélia / χέλια)

When you come across eels – peat brown, very slimy and about 50cms long – in the market, they will be attempting to escape from the bucket in which they have been kept since their removal from the lakes at Aghios Spiridon and Halicouna. Unfortunately, buying them live and squirming means you have to kill them: naturally, by leaving them out of water (not recommended) or by chopping their heads off. Corfiots like to make the stew *bourthéto* (see page 62) with smaller eels – larger ones are grilled.

Octopus

(Htapóthi / χταπόδι)

Did you know that an octopus is brainier (if less amenable) than a dog? Sometimes having a degree in zoology is a distinct disadvantage; I always find myself hoping that an octopus is already dead by the time it is thrashed to tenderness on some landing jetty. Properly cooked, octopus tastes rather like a cross between lobster and scallop; on Corfu, you are most likely to find it pickled or stewed.

Spiny lobster

(Astakos / αστακός)

Spiny lobster is found off the rocks in Paleocastritsa and Boukari; it is actually a different species from the 'real' lobster, as it doesn't have claws. But don't feel short-changed, as spiny lobster (or crawfish, as it is also known) tastes even better than the more famous 'Homard'. If you buy a live one, the most humane way to dispatch it is to freeze it for a couple of hours to render it comatose, before plunging it into rapidly boiling, salted water. Once cooked, don't mask its flavour with sauces: try serving it cold with homemade mayonnaise or oil and lemon juice.

In tavernas, you may come across 'pasta and lobster sauce' on the menu – this is the chef's way of making a small amount of meat go a very long way. The dressing will either be simple oil or butter, or tomato with a fish-stock base.

Scorpion fish

(Scorpios / σκορπιός)

These are rather ugly beasties, with spines that can cause a nasty swelling if you manage to impale yourself on them; their colour is variable but usually red or orange. Be warned; if you are not into bones, then you won't like scorpion fish. It tastes delicious, but you don't get much flesh from it, even if you are a whiz at dissection. Scorpion fish are usually made into a *bourthéto*, but you could also try baking it, remembering to baste it often.

How to clean and gut fish

As mentioned earlier, you're unlikely to find a fishmonger who will clean your purchase for you. But with a little determination, you'll find the task isn't nearly as gruesome as you might suppose, and fresh fish doesn't pong (promise).

Before you start, arm yourself with the following:

- A decent pair of scissors for trimming fins and cutting through gills

- A sturdy, sharp-bladed knife

- A heavy, solid chopping board. Now station yourself with the fish by the sink.

There are three steps to the operation: trimming, de-scaling and gutting.

Trimming means removing fins before you injure yourself – depending on the species of fish, the dorsal fins in particular can have nasty spines. Carefully cut away the dorsal, anal and pelvic fins flush to the body.

To de-scale, take the fish by the tail and place it under running cold water. Using the blunt side of the knife blade (the sharp side will result in a massacred fish), scrape the knife towards the head and make sure you remove every last scale. With small, oily fish such as anchovy, you might be able to do this with your thumbnail.

Then gut the fish. Start by making an incision by the anus; then insert the knife, sharp edge outwards, and pretend you are opening an envelope. Make the opening go all the way up to the lower jaw. Take a look inside: the guts are composed of intestine, liver and a green ball that is the gall bladder.

Gently pull the guts out of the cavity. Do not do anything to cause the gall bladder to rupture, as its contents are foul-tasting and will taint the fish. Cut the intestine at the throat as near to the gills as you can. Snip the other end at the anus and discard immediately.

Now wash the cavity thoroughly in cold water. Inside, you will see what looks like a tiny blood vessel running along the length of the spine. This is the kidney; remove it by taking the tip of the knife – or your fingernail – and scraping it away from the bone. Rinse the cavity again.

Corfiots think the best tasting flesh is found in the fish's head. So if, like them, you are going to cook it whole, it is a good idea to remove the gills – they deteriorate very quickly – by using the scissors and cutting through where they attach to the head and mouth.

Finally, pat the fish dry and either cook it immediately or place, covered, in the coldest part of the refrigerator. Now reward yourself with a glass of wine.

Squids in

Cleaning squid is quite fun, but very different from cleaning a straightforward fish.

First pull the head (with its tentacles) from the body/sac. The two parts of the animal come apart very easily: it doesn't require brute force. The innards will come away with the head. Then remove the plasticky quill from inside the body cavity. Pull off the two fins at the base, then peel away the thin, beige-pink skin. Rinse inside and out. Return to the head, and feel with your fingers for the point where it becomes soft

– just in front of the eyes – then cut the tentacles off at this point. Squeeze the mouth-part, or beak, out from the centre of the tentacles and discard both it and the head. If the tentacles are large, cut them into bite-size pieces.

The body is now ready for stuffing (see the recipe on page 71). If you want to fry it, either cut it into rings or slit down one side to open it out into a flat piece, then lightly score diagonal lines in what was the inside of the sac to make a diamond pattern.

Vegetables

One of the benefits of tourism is that there is now a broader range of produce on offer in the shops and markets. For example, the salad-leaf rocket is readily available, thanks to the Italian contingent of the August tourist influx. But whatever vegetables you choose, don't be afraid to feel and smell before you buy – the Corfiots do.

Aubergine

(Melitzánes / μελιτζάνες)

For the food historians amongst you, the aubergine was not a vegetable that was used a great deal on Corfu prior to the tourist invasion, although of course it is now available year round. Thus most of the recipes for aubergine originate from other parts of Greece.

Choose vegetables so plump that they look as if they are about to burst out of their skins. Size does not affect taste, so select ones on the basis of the recipe you have in mind.

Artichokes

(Angináres / αγκινάρες)

When artichokes first appear on sale in spring, they are the size of large walnuts and do not have a hairy choke at their centre.

All you have to do with them is add them to the recipe of your choosing. Through the summer they get progressively larger, but whatever the size, don't buy artichokes that have limp stalks – this indicates that they were harvested some while previously and will not be at their best. The stalk beneath the artichoke, up to about 4cms in length, is also edible. With older plants you may need to peel this section.

And if you've ever wondered why wine tastes pretty filthy when you are drinking it alongside artichokes, here's the explanation. It's because it contains a naturally occurring chemical called cynarin, which sweetens the flavour of the next thing that is put into your mouth.

Beetroot

(Kokkinogoúli / κοκινογούλι)

Beetroots only make an appearance in the markets in autumn and winter. They are sold with the leaves still attached, which give a good guide to freshness – they should still be crisp and not in any way wilted. Beetroot leaves can be blanched (if the tough stems are removed first) and used along with the roots in a salad. In spring, you can sometimes find just the young beet greens for sale.

Broad beans

(Kookyá / κουκκιά)

Broad beans have been part of the Mediterranean diet for over 5,000 years. Dried broad beans are easily available year round for use in purées and soups, but the season for fresh beans is a short one.

In early spring, the pods can be cooked whole. They should be the size of a finger to do this. When the pod has grown a little larger, the beans inside are the size of a little fingernail and can be eaten raw. Fully developed beans have a tough grey skin, which is best removed after boiling to reveal the pretty, emerald-green kernel within.

Broad bean and artichoke casserole is one of the one of the most delectable of Greek vegetable dishes; try the recipe on page 60.

Cabbage

(Krambí / κραμπί)

A popular vegetable in Corfu. The most common variety is large and white, and is excellent stuffed for *dolmades* or turning into a coleslaw-type salad. *Krambí* is sometimes given the red-sauce treatment, stewed to tenderness with paprika and tomato. Savoy and red cabbage are also available in season.

Incidentally, in the rest of Greece white cabbage is called *láhano*, but in Corfu this simply means 'vegetable'.

Courgettes

(Kolokythákia / κολοκυθάκια)

In the market, the more expensive courgettes are, the fresher they will be. Sometimes they are sold with their flowers still attached; if you try buying them like this early in the morning, you may find bees still inside the flower – so chose carefully. The flowers wilt very rapidly; if you are not going to use them immediately, remove them.

There are several ways to cook courgette flowers. They can be dunked in batter and then fried; stuffed, battered and fried; or stuffed and baked – a whole chapter could be written on the subject. If you are going to attempt one or all of these variations, your task will be helped enormously by placing the flowers petal-side down on a work surface, with the petals splayed outwards. This stops them from closing up and marginally reduces the fiddle factor.

French beans

(Fasolákia / φασολάκια)

Fasolákia are French green beans and they are turned into an excellent stew found in some tavernas. Test a bean for freshness by bending it: the fresher it is the more quickly it will snap. The really thin green beans are called *fasolákia velónes* – the latter word means 'needle' in Greek.

Peppers

(Piperiés / πιπεριές)

Thirty years ago the only capsicum available commercially was the green bell pepper. I dislike the bitterness of this variety, which is still used for stuffing in practically every taverna in Greece, but never mind, for more

recently there has been an explosion in the varieties for sale. Nowadays you can buy yellow and red bell peppers; Hungarian-style, long, pointed red and yellow ones; and a pale yellow-green pointed pepper that makes an excellent substitute for the Dreaded Green Bell.

The peppers used to make the paprika and cayenne pepper spice so beloved by Corfiots aren't grown locally, as the climate is neither hot or dry enough.

Potatoes

(Patátes / πατάτες)

Waxy varieties are more commonly for sale than floury types – all the better to make salads with – but it is a matter of 'buy and see' to find out which category the potatoes belong to. It is difficult to be more precise than this as the habit of naming varieties has yet to catch on in Corfu.

As with a lot of other vegetables, potatoes will not have been treated to stop sprouting, so buy only what you need for the next couple of days. And don't be put off by soil clinging to spuds, as this will have protected them from bruising and greening.

While we're on the subject of potatoes, everyone working in a resort taverna will know the word 'chips', having been dishing them up to tourists for the last 30 years. If you find yourself off the beaten track and fancy a plateful, the Greek for chips is *patátes tiganités*.

Tomatoes

(Tomátes / τομάτες)

The best tomatoes are ones that have come from plants left in a vegetable patch in full sun and only given just enough water to keep them healthy. In other words, they are stressed-out. And they taste wonderful as a

result. Unfortunately, this isn't a commercially viable proposition, so most Greek tomatoes are greenhouse grown.

Be careful when selecting tomatoes. Keep a look out for bruising and bollworm damage – the evidence for the latter is a small round black hole. Tomatoes are picked two to three days before they are ripe so, once you have bought some; keep them or a day or so.

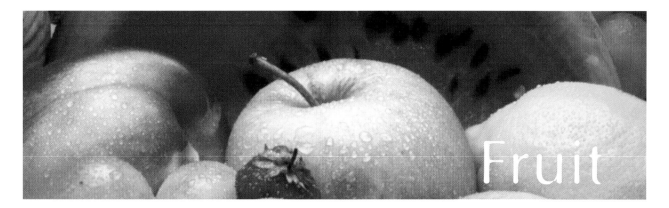

Fruit

The climate in Corfu allows a wide range of fruit to grow, from citrus to strawberries. But there is not much in the way of commercial production, at least partly because Corfu's rainfall is higher than the average for Greece, which increases the chances of fruit becoming blemished. The great advantage for consumers is that because locally grown fruit hasn't had to travel, it hasn't been picked 'green' and artificially ripened – so it tastes much nicer. You have to be careful though, as a lot of fruit is imported from Italy and mainland Greece. If you want to know where the fruit you are buying comes from, check the cardboard or wooden box it comes in – most fruit is sold still in its packing tray.

Figs

(Syka / συκα)

In Corfu, fig trees are arboreal weeds. They seed everywhere and are devilishly difficult to get rid of: their extensive root system, designed to absorb nutrients and water from dry, difficult soils, is almost impossible to dig out. Consequently they are a common sight, growing out of walls and other inaccessible places.

Locals don't bother naming the varieties: figs are figs. Everybody has access to a tree, which is a good thing because they don't travel well. There are two basic types, black and green; these can be subdivided into large and small. Not too tricky. All you need to remember is: large black figs make the sweetest eating if you like them raw; small green ones are usually used for making preserves and *sykópittes* (see page 20).

If you are entertaining, baked figs make an easy pudding: simply put the fruit – allow about three per person – into a dish large enough to accommodate them all in single layer. Slosh some decent Metaxa brandy over them, sprinkle with the zest of a lemon and a tablespoon of its juice, tuck a couple of bay leaves in between the figs, and bake in a hot oven for around 25 minutes.

Grapes

(Stafília / σταφύλια)

Practically every home on the island has a vine trained over a patio to provide both fruit and shade. These local varieties can often be thick skinned and 'pippy', but taste deliciously sweet. The kinds of grapes on sale in the shops change through the summer.

The season starts with Thompson Seedless – a white grape with smallish golden fruit that, left to dry, turns into sultanas. The Muscat grape appears next and local varieties come to market last of all, at the same time as winemaking starts.

The red strawberry grape – '*fraoula*' in Greek – is so-named because of its flavour. This is a table and a wine grape and has an unusual, slightly pungent after-taste. You have been warned.

Kumquats

(Kumkuat / κουμκουάτ)

Platanos is the main area for growing kumquats (*Citrus japonica*). Kumquat skin is sweet and the flesh is sour. It was introduced to Corfu when the island was still under British rule and today is the only fruit actively marketed on the island. It is converted into a virulent orange liqueur that is sold to tourists in bottles of all sorts of bizarre shapes and sizes. There is also a colourless, more expensive version: the one bought by Corfiots.

Homemade kumquat liqueur is less sweet and sickly than the commercial version, and is very easy to make. You'll need to take a kilo of the fruit back home with you after your holiday. Wash, then prick them all over before putting equal amounts into suitable glass jars with tight-fitting lids. Distribute half a kilo of sugar between the jars and top them up with two bottles of vodka (don't use gin, as these days its alcohol content is reduced and the juniper flavouring will interfere the taste of the kumquat). Seal the jar. Leave for six months, giving the jars a good shake from time to time. Decant. Use the (very slightly tinted) liqueur in fruit salads, with ice cream, or as an after-dinner digestif.

Lemons

(Lemónia / λεμόνια)

Lemons are nearly always local. They often have thick skins, because of the island's winter cold, and may be a bit marked. But don't let that put you off – they are still very juicy. Check for the leaves for freshness and use them quickly. Lemon juice has been used since the Greeks first started cultivating the fruit centuries ago, and so is a keynote flavour in Greek cuisine.

Melons

(Pepónia / πεπόνια)

and watermelons

(Karpoúzi / καρπούζι)

Both watermelons and 'musk' melons are in plentiful supply throughout the summer months, but the quality is rather variable. Before buying a melon of any variety, pick it up: it should feel heavy for its size. Then press the stem end, which should give a little; this tells you that it is ripe. Give it a good sniff to check for a heady, sweet aroma. Finally check for bruising – a sign that the fruit has been handled badly – which you can spot by depressions in the skin.

Watermelons are usually so large they are cut in half, not only for display purposes but also because a whole one is too much for one meal. If you do buy a whole one, tap it: it should sound hollow because its flesh is so plump full of water. If it is cut, make sure the seeds are black and the flesh is a vibrantly deep pink (an indicator of sweetness).

Don't store honeydew and cantaloupe melons in the fridge: they will taint everything else in it.

Mulberries

(Moúra / μούρα)

Mulberries make a brief appearance in the markets in early June, though as they are not grown commercially the punnets that appear are usually the surplus from somebody's tree. As the berries ripen, they turn from green to pink to a deep purple. They will continue to ripen once picked and will therefore keep a few days if kept cool.

Mulberries are delicious stewed with a little water and sugar, and spooned over yoghurt. Try not to dribble: mulberry juice is an impossible stain to remove from clothing.

Oranges

(Portokália / πορτοκάλια)

Greek oranges are delicious. The skin is soft and uneven in thickness so the fruit damages rather easily and, as a consequence, you won't see them in the supermarkets in northern Europe. A large proportion of the country's crop is grown on the mainland in an area stretching from Arta all the way south to Agrinio; because the oranges do not travel well, most of them end up as juice.

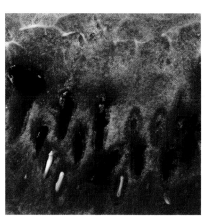

Corfiot oranges are in season from December until around April, but mainland oranges are available until the early summer. They are often sold with some leaves still attached; when buying them, check that the leaves are green and crisp to be sure the fruit is still fresh.

Oranges will not have been waxed or washed with fungicide to prevent wilting, so don't buy more than you need for a couple of days or you run the risk of them beginning to fizz. Not that there's much chance of that: they are so wonderfully sweet that the fruit bowl will soon be empty.

Seville oranges, in the form of peel or a small whole green orange, also make an appearance, candied and then covered in chocolate.

Peaches

(Rothákina / ροδάκινα)

and apricots

(Veríkoka / βερίκοκα)

The season for locally grown fruit is very short – you'll find them in the shops from early May to June. The rest of the year they are imported from Italy and the mainland. Let price be your guide.

Pears

(Ahláthia / αχλάδια)

and apples

(Míla / μήλα)

These fruit are nearly all imported. The local, brightly coloured yellow and red pear needs to be cooked first before being eaten, as when raw it is nearly inedible.

Quince

(Kithóni / κιδώνι)

The quince is the symbol of love, happiness and fertility for the Greeks. Its delicate blossom is a pale pink and the fruit itself smells gorgeous, so you have an inkling why it has this favoured status. However, they do not ripen until October and are not grown commercially in Corfu, so you will need to be lucky, or determined, to find the fruits in the market. If you do, only choose bright yellow fruit, rather than those still tinged with green, and check for insect holes. Quinces also bruise easily, so handle with care and do not refrigerate.

The usual fate for quinces are to be turned into a preserve or baked, perhaps with a sweet wine and spices such as cinnamon.

Herbs and spices

Corfiots are very keen on herbs for both culinary and medicinal reasons. They also like to grow their own and gather them from the countryside (see Nature's Bounty, opposite). But plenty of herbs and spices are also commonly available in the shops.

Basil
(Vasilikós / βασιλικός)
Every windowsill and veranda in Corfu bears a pot of basil. The variety that is most common has tiny leaves – ideal for scattering over salads – and grows into an attractive pom-pom shape. You won't find it for sale in the supermarkets, however, because it is not used that much in cooking; look for it in a garden centre or market instead.

Celery leaf
(Sélino / σέλινο)
Sélino has slightly larger leaves than parsley, and is good to use in casseroles and sauces, adding depth to the usual mix of oil, onion and garlic. It also gets round the usual objection people have to 'normal' celery – its stringy texture.

Cinnamon
(Kanélla / κανέλλα)
Cinnamon is another popular spice that makes an appearance in stews and pasta sauces, as well as sprinkled over sweet dishes such as semolina pudding cake or doughnuts.

Dill
(Ánitho / άνηθο)
Apparently this herb was so highly valued by the ancient Romans, they put a tax on it. Dill is quite a strong-tasting herb and if fennel fronds are available, you could try these as a superior substitute. Dill is a key ingredient in spring vegetable stews.

Parsley
(Maindanós / μαϊντανός)
A handful of chopped parsley finds its way into most Corfiot savoury dishes. It is usually available all the year round, but be aware that it is easily confused with *sélino*, the celery herb (see left) that is also used a lot in local dishes.

Pot marjoram, or oregano
(Rigani / ριγανη)
Dried rigani is used more commonly than fresh. The dried herb is usually sold in clear, square, plastic boxes (but see page 41 for how to find and make your own).

Red pepper (paprika and cayenne)
(Kokkino piperí / κοκκινο πιπερι)
Red pepper is a spice that Corfiots are really keen on. The rest of the Ionians don't use it and there are various theories about why this is so: Balkan connections, refugee influence and so forth. Whatever the history, bear in mind there are two varieties and check the packet before buying it:

glyko (γλυκό)	'soft' pepper, or paprika
kaftero (καυτερό)	cayenne pepper

The sauce in **bourthéto** stew (see page 62) uses red pepper. Some cooks insist the only pepper to use is cayenne, others suggest a mixture – it is all a matter of personal preference.

Nature's bounty

Corfu is rich in wild food that is just there for the picking. However, in the interests of conservation and keeping on the right side of the law, remember that the hunt is perhaps more important than the harvest. So:

- If a fruit or plant looks like it might belong to someone, ask permission before helping yourself. A fig tree, for example, will always have an owner, no matter how remote its location.

- Be very sparing and cautious in how you gather something, whether plant or animal. Don't pull plants up by the roots, don't disturb natural habitats.

This may seem self-evident, but you'd be amazed at how haphazard people can be. End of lecture.

The seashore

Should you go down to the seashore today, you are in for a nice surprise: both rock pools and sand dunes are full of edible treats.

Mantis shrimp

(Kanókes / κανόκες)

Mantis shrimps are weird-looking things – a sort of cross between a giant, flattened woodlouse and a prawn, although

taxonomically speaking this analogy is very inaccurate. Anyway, in March, when they are at their best, try netting them in shallow waters, or resort to your friendly fish-seller. Cook them as you would ordinary shrimp and be prepared for a fiddle getting rid of the carapace and the rest of its armoury (what do you do with an animal that has a pair of legs coming out of its mouth?). Equip yourself with a huge napkin and roll up your sleeves: the meat will be your reward.

Prawns

(Garíthes / γαρίδες)

I am not sure you will ever gather enough from the wild to make a meal out of them, but hunting for prawns is a splendid way of keeping young children occupied. Search for these semi-transparent crustacea in seawater rock pools just after the tide has gone out. A more convenient habitat is the supermarket deep-freeze.

A popular way of cooking prawns that sometimes appears on taverna menus is called *garíthes youvetsi*: baked with tomato sauce and feta cheese. To make this yourself, shell around five prawns per person (raw, if possible, as they are less likely to overcook

and toughen). Make a very thick tomato sauce using garlic, white wine, parsley and the fullest-flavoured fresh tomatoes you can find. Then put the prawns at the bottom of an earthenware pot and spoon over the sauce until they are completely submerged in tomato. Cover with slices of feta and bake in a very hot oven for 15 minutes.

Rock samphire

(Chrithum maritimum)

Not the same species as that found in northern European waters, this samphire grows to about 15-30cm in height, with fleshy, multi-branched, narrow and segmented bluish-green leaves, and pale yellow umbels of flowers in summer. Gather it from coastal rocks and sand dunes in early spring – before it becomes tough – and pick only that which is within reach of the sea's spray. Nibble a bit first to see if you like the taste and if so, pick enough to eat it as a relish; a little goes a long way as the flavour, a sort of aromatic iodine, is quite strong. To cook, simply blanch it and serve with grilled fish or a risotto.

Sea urchins

(Ahinós / αχινός)

The local population is struggling to keep its numbers up, partly because the waves from fast passenger ferries tend to suck them up from the sea bed and smash them against the rocks, and partly because just about everyone but the British regards them as a delicacy on a par with caviare.

You will find sea urchins in rock pools and shallow waters; hunt for them only when there is a full moon (when the urchins are full of roe), and be sparing about how many you collect. You eat them raw: cut the top open like a boiled egg, rinse them in the sea to clean their gut out (they are herbivorous grazers so the contents are nothing too awful) and scoop out the roe. Squeeze a couple of drops of lemon juice over them, and devour.

Whitebait

(Maridáki / μαριδάκι)

Whitebait is the generic term for very small fish, usually from the mackerel family. One is only allowed to fish for them between October and March. During this time of year you will notice people on the beaches standing knee deep in the water, hauling in their catch with nets.

The countryside

Asparagus

(Sparángia / σπαράγγια)

Wild asparagus looks like a spindly version of cultivated asparagus and is highly appreciated by Corfiots, though the ancient Greeks did not like it very much: they claimed 'it makes one barren and not fit for generation' (possibly because it makes pee smell terrible). It is about the only plant that can grow through olive nets, so it is easy

to spot heading skywards through the months of March and April. Pick the top 10cms or so of the stem and boil in large quantities of water until tender (unlike cultivated asparagus, it needs this treatment or it can be very bitter).

Bay

(Dáphni / δάφνη)

A plant rich with cultural associations. The Greek name comes from the nymph of legend, who the gods turned into a tree to stop naughty old Apollo chasing her. He felt guilty about this and declared the tree sacred, after which anyone with any importance wore a wreath of it as a symbol of honour. It was also used to ward against bad luck and illness, while today Corfiots use its branches for making walking sticks, and strew its leaves over church floors whenever a village celebrates its saint's day.

You may be used to seeing it in pots, pruned into geometric shapes, but left to its own devices it is a large shrub that can be well over 2m high. It grows all over the island in gullies and thickets; if you want to snip a twig to keep to hand in the kitchen, the best time to do this is at the end of the summer when the new growth has had a chance to harden off.

Capers

(Kápari / κάπαρη)

Capers are the unopened flower buds of a rather nondescript plant called 'Kaparis spinosa' that straggles over the rock slopes of Mt Pantecrator. The leaves are oval, but the best way to recognise it is by its flower (though by this time it is too late to pick capers for pickling), which has lots of long, delicate mauve stamens surrounded by white or pale pink petals. If you do come across some buds, check for signs of

resident or visiting insect life. Then all you need to do is rinse and dry them before packing them in sea salt for two days. Either leave them like this, or rinse and pop them into glass jars topped up with Greek red-wine vinegar.

Chicory

(Radíkia / ραδίκια)

Corfiots pick the leaves for *hórta* (see right), while the roots are also edible if soaked for a day before boiling. Dioscirides, the father of herbal medicine, decided chicory was – amongst other things – an aphrodisiac. Look for cornflower-blue, daisy-like flowers on an untidy, straight-stemmed plant over a metre tall.

Dandelion

(Picralítha / πικραλίδα)

Immediately recognisable from its ubiquity on suburban lawns back home, the dandelion is closely related to chicory and, like chicory, its roots can be eaten as well as turned into a coffee substitute. Use only the youngest leaves for a *hórta* or salad. And don't eat too much, as it is a diuretic.

Giant fennel and wild fennel

(Márathos / μάραδος)

This herb goes very well with fish. If you haven't got any fennel growing in your garden, use the leafy fronds from vegetables in the market.

Fennel (both species) is a member of the cow parsley family and its flowers, though yellow, are similar. So is its shape, which is large and straggly. Incidentally, Bacchus, god of wine, recommended that his followers used fennel branches for sticks so that when they got drunk they would not end up injuring themselves in brawl.

Pot marjoram, aka oregano

(Rigani / ριγανή)

'A salad without *rigani* is dead,' is the firmly held view of most Corfiots and, indeed, what would a Corfiot meal be without its dusting of these dried flower heads? (Even though one can use them fresh, Corfiots prefer dried, and the leaves are considered too bitter.)

The herb is very common, growing to about 30cm in meadows, roadsides and olive groves, with tiny white clusters of flowers towards the top of the plant. Stems should be cropped in early June and, traditionally, tied together in a posy before being left to dry upside down in a shady spot.

Rosemary

(Dendrolívano / δεντρολίβανο)

Though not indigenous, rosemary grows everywhere on the island. Yet it occupies the same place in Corfiot cuisine as lavender does in British: that is to say, it is rarely used, regarded as something of an oddity, and is more likely to be used in linen water. Try making rosemary-infused olive oil, by snipping the leaves into the oil, perhaps with a clove of garlic, and leaving it to infuse for a week or so.

Sloes

(Korómilo / κορόμηλο)

If you go hiking across the Troumpetta Pass in autumn, look out for these small blue-black fruit; but be careful how you pick them, as the sloe bush has long thorns. To make sloe gin, mix the berries with half their weight in sugar and half-fill the requisite number of bottles. Top up with gin and add a cinnamon stick to each. Seal tightly and leave for a minimum of two months. You'll find sloe gin keeps for years.

Sweet chestnut

(Kástana / κάστανα)

Roasted chestnuts are sold on street corners in Corfu Town in the autumn. The trees grow in sheltered valleys and the spiny pom-poms are easy to spot from September onwards. The fruit tend to be a bit wormy, so if you want to keep them, remove their casings and check them over carefully before drying them in an oven at about 50C for an hour or so to kill off any remaining wildlife. If roasting them immediately, make an incision in the side of each chestnut, except for one. Put this unslit one into the hot coals along with the others; when it explodes you'll know the chestnuts are ready.

Wild strawberries

(Ágries fraoúles / φράουλες)

Corfu was once famous for its wild strawberries, which it used to export before tourism became the most lucrative industry on the island. Look for them in early June in rocky, partly shady places and eat them as soon as possible, as they go bad very quickly (an over-ripe wild strawberry has a weird, boiled-sweet taste). They need no adornment, not even cream, although you may have to sprinkle them over yoghurt to make them go further.

Home is where the *hórta* is

Hórta, or wild greens, basically means anything green and edible that grows in the hills, including dandelion, chicory and sorrel. From December until the sun dries out the vegetation in May or June, people wander around with plastic bags collecting their favourite leaves. The best way to learn to recognise the different species is to get hold of a decent botanical field guide – or make friends with a passing plastic-bag carrier.

There are two common methods of dealing with *hórta*. Simply boiling them isn't always successful as they can end up as a chlorophyll cowpat; a local way is to sauté them with lots of red pepper.

Booze

If you back-packed round Greece as a student and occasionally splashed out on a bottle of 'Domestos' or, if you were feeling very extravagant, Lac du Roches, you probably think Greek wines don't get any better. Think again. Greeks have been making wine for several thousand years, the country boasts around 250 indigenous grape varieties, and Greece is one of the hot newcomers to the wine scene.

Corfiot wine

Most wine books, if they mention Corfu at all, will tell you that the island should not be considered as a destination for the wine tourist. This may be true: tourism took a hold of the island before the wine renaissance began in Greece. Yet there are two winemaking areas on the island, around Liapades and Strinilas in the north and Lefkimmi in the south. Here wine is made on a co-operative basis: everyone's grapes go into a central pot, and the resulting wine is delivered in barrels to supermarkets and tavernas for immediate local consumption. So you may find that your nearest supermarket features something that looks like a cold-water dispenser; in fact it contains the local wine. Use it to fill a two litre empty

soft-drink bottle – don't forget to rinse it out first – chill and drink within 48 hours.

There is also a vineyard in Halikouna, in the south west of Corfu, whose eponymous wine has a *vin de pays* classification and is sold bottled through the supermarkets and wine merchants. It is a white, dry but honey-tasting, and deserves to be better known.

Quite apart from commercial wine-making, every Corfiot male over 15 is mad about making their own – it is ingrained in the national psyche. (This applies to taverna-owners, too, so it is always worth asking tavernas if they have any *krassi*, or local wine, which will arrive at the table in quarter or half-litre aluminium pitchers.) These days most people don't have the time to tend a vineyard, so every October you will see lorries lining the roads into Corfu Town selling nothing but grapes. And if you are an autumn visitor, watch out for wine-making festivals.

Wines from the rest of Greece

Really good wines come from all over Greece. At the budget end of the spectrum it is easier to find a palatable white than red,

which tend to be a bit thin. Better wines are relatively expensive – there is no added advantage to drinking the best wines that Greece has to offer in Corfu rather than, say, London, as along with the rest of the world, the island is an export market. Of course, you do get a broader range to choose from than your local off-licence.

The mega-wine producers – Boutari, Cambas, Tsantalis and Kourtakis – all churn out cheap but gluggable blended wines: Lac du Roches; Makedonikos; Apelia; and Calligas. You will have no trouble finding these – not only do these wines take up most of the space in the supermarket wine section, they also come in the biggest bottles and sport labels in English. Possibly the best at this budget end of the market is Attikos, which is a dry but fruity and fresh-tasting wine.

These producers also make more upmarket, varietal grape and estate-produced wines. Boutari has the biggest range. For everyday, dependable drinking try its red, medium-bodied Naoussa Grand Reserve. Moschofilero is its well-rounded white; once opened, a bottle never seems to last long.

The Zitsa wine co-operative, a two-hour drive away on the mainland, produces white wines that aren't too alcoholic, so they are ideal for a midday tipple. Look out for the off-dry, lightly bubbling 'Petilliant' style, and try drinking it with half a mint leaf added to the glass. Katogi Averoff , a winery from the same region as Zitsa, makes both white and red wines, such Traminer and Cabernet Sauvignon, which go well with meals.

The following is a small selection of other wines that are readily available in most supermarkets in Corfu. If you come across a winner, let everyone know via our The Taste of a Place website (see page 82 for details).

Posh or not

Some of the really smart boutique wineries make wonderful everyday wines, in addition to their 'serious' output:

- Antonopoulos makes Cabernet-Nea Dris, which is one of Greece's top red wines; its Collection (an unoaked chardonnay) and Mantinia whites are more affordable

- Gaia's upmarket wines include a fab white called Thalassitis, whilst their mid range red and white wines are marketed under the Notios label

- Ktima Mercouri, well known for its classy reds, also makes Foloe, a deliciously crisp, lemony white

- Kostas Lazaridis makes the red and white Amethystos wines that are very much in vogue, as well as and the marginally less expensive Chateau Julia range of whites – try the Assyrtiko.

Bin ends

Choose these for good value for money:

- Kokotos Thyoni: a quaffable white Moschifilero blend

- Oenoforos Asprolithi: a fragrant dry white, best before a meal

- Spyropoulos Mantinia: does well with chicken and pasta

- Skouras Cabernet Sauvignon: an ideal accompaniment to a steak or casserole

Other Greek booze

Retsina

Whatever you do, do not a) keep a bottle of retsina for a special occasion or b) think that it will improve with age. Retsina is a wine for immediate consumption which used to be taken direct to Athenian bars, where it would ferment in barrels on the premises.

Its characteristic pine-resin taste stems from (yup, you've guessed it) pine resin being added to wine back in antiquity, as it was thought then that this acted as a preservative. Actually it was the airtight seals on the casks that kept wine from going off but, by the time they worked this out, the Greeks had developed a taste for the stuff.

Retsina is still sold in draught form – see page 18 of our Culinary Tour for a suggestion of where to buy it in Corfu Town – and it's vital you buy it from an outlet with a fast turnover. The most commonly available retsina in Corfu is made by Kourtakis, who produce two brands – the crown-top and the yellow label. The latter is the more upmarket version.

Ouzo

A clear, aniseed-flavoured spirit made from grapes which turns cloudy if you add water to it. However, if you aspire to street-cred and want hairs on your chest, drink the water from a separate glass as the Greeks do.

Dedicated slurpers

If you want to find out more about Greek wine, then it helps to know what to look for on the labels. Otherwise it could take you several (very nice) bottles of white wine to figure out that Mantinia is a fashionable wine region in the Peloponnese – not a grape variety.

There are 28 'Appellations of Origin' (AoO) in Greece. This term is a means of classifying wine not just by physical location but also – amongst other things – by the type of grapes used and the vinification methods. The most commonly found AoO to be found on Corfiot supermarket shelves include:

- **Mantinia** (Peloponnese)
- **Naoussa** (Macedonia)
- **Nemea** (Peloponnese)
- **Patras** (Peloponnese)
- **Robola of Cephalonia** (Ionian Islands)
- **Zitsa** (Epirus)

Be aware that some of Greece's best wines do not meet the criteria for being marketed as an Appellation of Origin. And there is also a *vin de pays* classification, which is not quite so strict.

Great grapes

If you want to explore the 45 or so indigenous grape varieties currently being experimented with in Greece, then here are some names that you might also see on the label:

White grape cultivars

Assyritiko has been around for several thousand years. It is made into a range of styles, including the sweet Vinsantos, and grows mostly on Santorini (home to several good wine producers) and the Cyclades.

Athiri wines tend to have a high alcohol content and low acidity. It is quite often blended with other varieties, particularly Assyritiko.

Kakotryghis means 'hard to cut' as the stems are tough. It is native to Corfu and is the grape used to make Halicouna. It results in a honey-tasting, dark yellow wine.

Lagorthi came close to extinction but it now appears in some very trendy wines.

Moschofilero is grown mostly in the Mantinia region and makes a very pleasant, 'drink on its own' wine.

Robola is found mostly on the Ionian Islands, in particular, Cephalonia; it has a lemony taste and is quite often blended with other cultivars.

Red wine cultivars

Aghiorghitiko is a very popular variety that is usually blended with other cultivars to produce wines ranging from the 'everyday dependable' to 'special occasion'.

Limnio grapes are used, in small amounts, in blends from some prestigious producers. It has been around since ancient times and probably originated from the island of Lemnos where, ironically, it does not grow very well: it is happier in northern Greece.

Mavrodaphne means 'black laurel' and it is usually used to produce a dessert wine.

Volitza Mavri is a cultivar still very much being experimented with and so is grown in only very small quantities.

Xinomavro is an important variety found in northern Greece, and is the varietal required to produce Naoussa and Goumenissa wines. The grape produces a versatile and full-bodied wine.

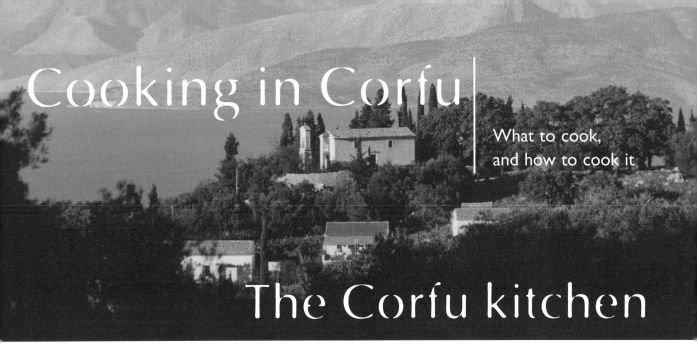

Cooking in Corfu

What to cook, and how to cook it

The Corfu kitchen

Some people hate cooking on holiday. Others only occasionally venture forth to a taverna because they are having such fun in the kitchen. But wherever you are on the spectrum, there are going to be evenings or lunches when you will find yourself eating in. And the trouble with a lot of holiday homes is that, no matter how well appointed the rest of the house, the owners or developers run out of enthusiasm when it comes to equipping the kitchen. Even if the tools, bowls and equipment began life in an OK condition, after a couple of seasons of – for example – the knife being used as a tin-opener, the contents of the cupboards will look like the leftovers from a car-boot sale.

So it is best to come prepared. Personally, I never go on holiday without a very sharp knife, a decent penknife with a bottle / tin opener, tweezers (useful for fish bones) and a corkscrew – there is nothing worse than staring at a bottle of wine that you can't open. (Obviously, post 9/11, these are all

packed in my suitcase.) You could even consider sacrificing your hairdryer and pack a hand-held whizzer instead, for those enthused moments when you decide to make hummus and would prefer not to use a potato masher to pulverise chickpeas.

The really forward-thinking may want to ring their tour operator to enquire about the state of the kitchen. But whatever the state of your holiday kitchen, you'll find something suitable to cook in the following chapters.

All of the recipes use ingredients that are readily available in Corfu; some are typically Corfiot; others are Greek; and several aren't Greek at all, just ones that I and my family use regularly.

Bear in mind you do not have to be too exact with your measurements; for many centuries, Greek housewives have got by without a set of scales, simply using sight and taste to guide them.

Key to symbols

 No cooking

 Gas or electric ring required

 Oven required

 Cooking to impress. For when you feel inspired – either on holiday or back home – to dazzle everyone with your culinary prowess

 Local speciality

All recipes are for approximately six people, unless otherwise stated. Whenever 'olive oil' is listed as an ingredient, it should be extra-virgin

Starters and dips

Aubergine Dip (Melitzanosaláta)

The best way of cooking an aubergine in preparation for a dip is to grill it over a gas ring or barbeque; this will give a wonderful smoky flavour to the 'salata'. In the absence of naked flame, the next best thing is to oil the skin and then bake the aubergine in an oven at 180C / 350F / Gas 4 for around 45 minutes. And if you are going to cook one, you may as well cook three, because the dip keeps for a couple of days in the refrigerator.

Some recipes call for grated onion, which is great if you want to declare the space around you a people-free zone. Spring onions are a friendlier option.

3 aubergines, roasted and peeled
3 spring onions, sliced finely including
   the green stalks
80ml olive oil
juice of a lemon
1 or more cloves garlic, mashed with salt
4 tbsps chopped parsley
salt and freshly ground pepper

Press the cooked aubergine flesh into a colander with a wooden spoon to extract the excess juices. Chop it up very finely, place in a bowl and mash in the garlic, followed by the parsley, spring onions and lemon juice. Gradually beat in the oil, as if you were making mayonnaise. Season with salt and pepper to taste.

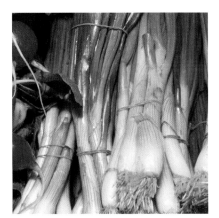

Fast tomato tart

Use ready-made puff pastry, and the most flavoursome tomatoes you can lay your hands on.

1kg tomatoes, cored, peeled and sliced
450g puff pastry
50g graviera cheese (see page 25), grated
50g képhalotyri cheese (see page 25), grated
bunch of basil, shredded
flour for dusting
olive oil
salt and freshly ground black pepper

Preheat the oven to 225C / 425F / Gas 7. Divide the pastry into three equal pieces and roll each portion out on a floured work surface until it's around 18 x 30cms. Then cut each square in half, to make six square pastry bases. Transfer to a couple of lightly oiled baking trays, and prick all over. Arrange the tomatoes over the squares so that they just overlap one another, but don't butt right up to the edge of the pastry; then brush with a little olive oil. Now tuck a few shredded basil leaves around and under the tomatoes, before muddling together the two grated cheeses and sprinkling half over the tomato slices. Season, dribble olive oil over everything, and pop the lot into the top of the oven for 15 to 20 minutes, or until the pastry under the tomatoes has cooked. Scatter over the rest of the grated cheese, and serve with a rocket salad.

Feta and pepper dip

A dip that also makes an excellent sandwich filling.

1 packet of feta (the sheep's milk variety)
2 roasted red peppers – from a jar is fine
1 sliced onion, sautéed in olive oil until soft
1 small tub of strained whole milk yoghurt
pinch of cayenne pepper

If you have a food processor, use the pulse button to mix everything together – it should have the texture of cottage cheese. Chill until needed.

Fasolákia

French beans stewed in olive oil and tomatoes is one of those dishes which tastes completely different home-cooked from those that appear on taverna menus. Greek cooks use far more olive oil and cook the beans for so long that they almost fall apart, but as you probably don't have access to your own olive oil, this version uses rather less than is traditional; it is still delicious. These days, fresh tomatoes rarely seem to be ripe or flavoursome enough for this recipe, so use the tinned, sieved type instead.

750g French beans, top, tailed, and snapped in half if necessary
250ml tin or box of sieved tomatoes
1 onion, finely chopped
3 or 4 cloves garlic, peeled and crushed
5tbsps olive oil
water
small bunch of sélino (see page 38), chopped
1 bay leaf
half a tsp sugar
pinch each of ground cinnamon and cloves
salt and freshly ground pepper

Pour enough oil into a large, heavy bottomed saucepan to cover its base. Heat gently, then add the chopped onions and fry until they turn translucent. Sprinkle the sugar over the onions and continue to cook, stirring occasionally, until they start to turn a light treacle colour. Add the garlic, tomatoes, herbs and spices, turn the heat down and simmer for around five minutes. Season, then add the beans; give them a good stir and leave to simmer gently, without a lid, for 30 minutes. (If the sauce looks like it's getting too thick, or starts to stick to the pan, splash in a little water.) Once the beans are thoroughly tender, remove from the heat and let them cool a little. When they're just tepid, drizzle over a tablespoon or so of olive oil and serve immediately.

Hummus

Bog-standard and easy to do. Never the less, you may not make it often enough to remember the recipe. Here it is, just in case.

250ml tin chick peas, drained of liquid
50ml olive oil
2 cloves crushed garlic
1 generous tbsp tahini (more if you wish)
1 tsp ground cumin
juice of a lemon
salt and freshly ground pepper

Whiz everything together in a blender or food processor; thin with water if necessary. (By the way, if you have trouble finding a jar of tahini, try looking for it in the 'baking supplies' section of your local supermarket.) The non-electrical method is either to scrunch the chickpeas through a sieve or crush them in a pestle and mortar, before adding the rest of the ingredients.

Leeks à la Grecque

You can do lots of different vegetables 'à la Grecque' – try this same recipe with mushrooms or cauliflower. With the latter, blanche the florets for five minutes first.

4 leeks, trimmed of tough greenery and sliced
400ml dry white wine
250ml water
50ml olive oil, plus extra for serving
handful of fennel tops, chopped
2 bay leaves
1 tsp coriander seeds, partially crushed
half a tsp black peppercorns, partially crushed
half a tsp salt
lemon juice to taste
2 heaped tbsp chopped parsley to serve

Put everything except the leeks, lemon juice and parsley into a pan and simmer for 10 minutes, with the lid on. Add the leeks and simmer for another 10-15 minutes. Remove the cooked leeks, retain the liquor and boil it hard until it has reduced by half. Pour it over the leeks; add more oil and a squeeze of lemon juice to taste. Leave to cool to room temperature, then scatter parsley over the top and serve with lots of crusty bread to mop up the juices.

Marinated fried fish

In the days before refrigeration, this recipe was a way of preserving fish; there are probably as many versions as there are households. Traditionally it's made with small fish, such as picarel (see page 31) or sardine, but you could also use fillets from larger fish.

1kg picarel, gutted and cleaned
   (for how to clean fish, see page 32)
150ml olive oil
100g seasoned flour

for the marinade:

400ml olive oil
200ml good quality Greek wine vinegar
100g sultanas
10 cloves garlic, peeled and finely chopped
3 bay leaves
2 rosemary twigs – each about 6cms long
1 tbsp fennel fronds
1 tbsp whole black peppercorns

Put the flour and the fish in a plastic bag and give a good shake. Shallow-fry the fish for two to three minutes on each side, until they are cooked. You will need to do this in several batches, putting the cooked ones on kitchen paper to drain. Let them cool completely.

Meanwhile, put all the marinade ingredients in a suitable pan and bring to a simmer – you don't want a boiling cauldron, just a nicely burping one – and cook until the garlic is soft. Put the fish in a covered dish suitable for the refrigerator and, while the marinade is still hot, pour it over until the fish is completely submerged. Chill for at least 48 hours, and bring to room temperature before serving.

Omelette with mint and feta cheese

You can make an omelette out of lots of left-over ingredients: ham, tomato, onion, roast ratatouille-style vegetables, you name it. This combination came about one Sunday evening. There were no fresh herbs in the fridge, but outside under the lemon tree lurked some mint…

4 eggs
50g feta, crumbled
1 tbsp chopped fresh mint
freshly ground black pepper
a generous knob of butter

Serves two

The trick with making omelettes is to heat the frying pan on a medium heat for a couple of minutes before adding butter – or olive oil if you prefer. If using butter it should fizz nicely as soon as it hits the hot surface.

While the frying pan is heating, whisk the eggs and season with pepper. Salt isn't necessary because feta is usually quite salty enough – taste it first to see. Add the butter to the pan, let it melt and then immediately pour in the egg mixture. Using a spatula or knife, repeatedly draw the eggs back from the edge of the pan, tilting it so that the egg mixture flows towards the edges and cooks evenly. Once a cooked base has formed, but while the eggs are still runny on top, sprinkle on the feta and mint. Leave to cook for a minute or so until the feta is soft and the omelette is tanned underneath. Fold onto a plate and serve immediately.

Taramosalata

There are hundreds of variations of this recipe; which you choose all depends on the kind of texture you want your dip to be. Some people use potato, others use a mixture of spuds and bread, while I use bread alone. Greek bread seems to work better than British bread, so if you want to make taramosalata back home, try and choose a loaf, such as ciabatta, which dries out quickly. Most importantly of all, though, use decent taramás (see page 26) to begin with.

175g taramás, broken into chunks and
  soaked in cold water for 30 minutes
100g stale white breadcrumbs
100ml olive oil
1 clove of garlic, crushed
juice of half a lemon
salt
cayenne pepper

Electric method: put the taramás, breadcrumbs, garlic and lemon juice in a food processor and start blending. Then dribble the oil into the mixture as if making mayonnaise, until you achieve a purée the consistency of thick cream (if it gets too thick, add a drop of water). Season with salt and add more a lemon juice as required. Serve with a dusting of cayenne pepper and slices of warm pitta bread.

Tzakziki soup

Thinned-down tzakziki makes a refreshing soup.

1 large cucumber, peeled and grated
800ml plain whole milk yoghurt –
  supermarkets sell it by weight at
  the deli counter
500ml very cold water
50g mint leaves, chopped
2 plump cloves of garlic, crushed with
a teaspoon of salt
squeeze of lemon juice to taste
cayenne pepper

Add the grated cucumber and garlic to the yoghurt, and stir thoroughly. Add water, stirring as you pour until you achieve the consistency of single cream. Season with lemon juice and cayenne to suit your taste buds. Keep in the fridge until ready to serve – then stir in the mint leaves.

Salads

Broad bean and graviera salad

If you have only been able to buy older (bigger) broad beans, this salad is much nicer if, after you have boiled the beans, you remove their skins. It may be a hassle but your reward is a salad that not only tastes yummy but looks very pretty too.

2kg broad bean pods
250g rocket leaves, with tough
   stalks removed
150g graviera cheese (see page 25),
   shaved or sliced very thinly
8 tbsp olive oil
1 bunch of sélino (see page 38), chopped
juice of a lemon

Pod the beans. If they are very small, the beans can be eaten raw; larger ones should be blanched in boiling, salted water for 3 to 5 minutes, then popped out of their skins if they are tough and grey. Coat with the olive oil and lemon juice whilst they are still warm, mix the rocket and sélino, and then stir through the beans. Scatter the cheese over the top of the salad and serve.

Cabbage salad with rigani

A Greek variant on the coleslaw theme.

400g 'lahano' cabbage (see page 33),
   very finely shredded
4 carrots, peeled and coarsely grated
2 Kos lettuces – or any other crisp lettuce –
shredded
6 tbsp olive oil
2 tsp Greek red wine vinegar
1 generous tsp Dijon mustard
1 small clove of garlic, crushed
1 bunch parsley, chopped
half a tsp dried rigani (see page 38)
half a tsp cayenne pepper
half a tsp sugar

Shake all the ingredients except the cabbage, carrots, parsley and lettuce in a jam jar. Taste and adjust the seasoning to suit. Pour the dressing over the cabbage, carrots and parsley, mix thoroughly and leave for 30 minutes or so. Stir in the lettuce just before serving.

Courgette salad

Blanching the courgettes is not essential, but means that they will absorb the dressing better.

1.5kg baby courgettes, halved or
   quartered if necessary
3 large spring onions, sliced into thin rounds
5 tbsp of olive oil
2 tbsp of chopped parsley
1 tbsp chopped sélino
1 tbsp capers, rinsed and chopped
1 tbsp lemon juice
salt and freshly ground black pepper

Blanche the courgettes by plunging in plenty of boiling, lightly salted water for two minutes, then draining and immediately rinsing in cold water. Mix with all of the remaining ingredients, and taste for seasoning before serving.

Cucumber and feta salad

 This recipe is based on the classic Greek salad – the tomatoes and olives are omitted because sometimes one can have too much of a good thing.

1 large cucumber, peeled and finely diced
3 large spring onions, sliced into thin rounds
150g feta, crumbled
5 tbsp of olive oil
2 tbsp of chopped fresh dill or fennel
1 tbsp lemon juice
salt if necessary

Mix all of the ingredients and check for salt just before serving.

No oil cucumber salad

 OK, this isn't even Greek, never mind Corfiot. But sometimes it is good to have a salad that 'cuts' the oil or fat present in any other salad(s) that you have rustled up. It is important to use decent wine vinegar – the Greek kind that comes in a small plastic bottle is fine.

1 large cucumber, peeled and finely sliced
1 tbsp sugar
1 tbsp wine vinegar
lemon juice (optional)
a handful of mint or parsley, chopped
salt and freshly ground black pepper

Put the cucumber in a sieve or colander and scatter generously with salt, then press down on the slices with a heavy bowl and leave for half an hour while the bitter juices drain away. Rinse through, pat dry if you are feeling dedicated, and pop in a serving dish.

Now dissolve the sugar in the vinegar – use a fork to whiz the liquid about – and add some lemon juice to taste if you feel like it. Stir this dressing and the mint or parsley through the cucumber, grind over some black pepper, and it's ready.

For a variation, dice rather than slice the cucumber, add a finely diced onion and a generous pinch of cayenne. The salad is now a salsa, and it goes very well with fish.

Fennel salad

 When fennel makes its first appearance in the spring, the vegetable is sold with its feathery leaves still attached. This salad makes the most of both the bulb and the fronds.

3 or 4 fennel bulbs
    (depending on their plumpness)
50g parmesan, képhalotyri or graviera cheese
    (see page 25)
olive oil
juice of a lemon and half a tsp of zest
a handful of Kalamata olives, pitted and
    roughly chopped, to serve

Remove the feathery leaves from the fennel, and chop finely. Discard any outer bits of the bulbs that look too tough or stringy. Slice, aiming for paper thinness. Throw into a suitable serving bowl. Pour over enough olive oil to anoint the slithers generously – I find using hands make the job of mixing much easier. Add the lemon juice, zest and chopped fennel fronds. Stir through and let the salad marinate for an hour or so. Just before serving, shave the cheese with a potato peeler, fold into the fennel and then scatter the olives over the top.

Green pepper and tomato salad

Use the slender, pale yellow-green, arthritic looking variety of peppers, which have a very faint chilli taste to them. The green bell pepper merely tastes bitter.

5 pale green peppers (or 3 of the darker
   green variety), cored and thinly sliced
4 tomatoes, diced, juices retained
1 spring onion, finely sliced
1 tbsp of basil leaves
Mustard Dressing (see page 75)
salt and freshly ground black pepper

Mix the ingredients, adjust the seasoning and serve. For a variation, add two finely chopped, hard-boiled eggs.

Hórta and caper salad

Collecting your own hórta (see page 41) is not essential; a mixture of leaves such as radicchio, chicory, lambs lettuce, sorrel, dandelion and rocket, from any source, will do.

1kg hórta, leaves washed and stripped
   from any tough stems
bunch sélino, (see page 38) coarsely
   chopped
2 lemons, zest removed and thinly sliced
2 tbsp capers, rinsed
1 tbsp freshly squeezed orange juice
olive oil
pinch of salt and cayenne pepper

Remove any excess pith from the lemon slices and then sprinkle with salt and cayenne. Leave until just before you're ready to serve, then add the lemon and any juice to a salad bowl in which you have mixed the greens, sélino, lemon zest and capers. Finally, add the orange juice and olive oil to taste.

Octopus salad

This is my brother's favourite salad. When he first gave me the recipe, he began with these instructions: find a flat rock, throw your octopus on the rock 80 times, and then rub it as you would laundry 80 times. Good news, gentle reader: you do not have to tenderise your octopus this way. Boiling it is much easier.

1kg small fresh octopi, cleaned
125ml olive oil
2 cloves of garlic
4 tbsp of chopped parsley
2 tbsp lemon juice
generous pinch salt

Boil the octopi for 20 to 45 minutes, or until they are tender. Drain and cut into small, mouthful-size pieces. Add the rest of the ingredients and leave to marinate for two hours. Accompany with a glass of ice-cold ouzo.

Peach and pepper salad

 I first saw a mention of this salad while in Kos – an island, it has be said, that doesn't have much going for it gastronomically speaking, in spite of having a lettuce named after it. I suspect this happy combination of flavours was originally Turkish.

For each person, allow:

*2 long red paprika peppers, washed, seeded
    and cut in quarters
half a peach, stoned, sliced, and skinned
    if you are feeling enthusiastic
4 tbsp olive oil
lemon juice to taste
half a tsp ground cumin
pinch cayenne pepper
salt and freshly ground black pepper*

Put the sliced peppers into a shallow roasting tray, pour over the olive oil, sprinkle on a pinch of salt and pepper, and mix thoroughly (clean hands are the best utensil). Bake in a pre-heated oven (190C / 375F / Gas 5) for 35 minutes or so until the peppers' skins are wilted and the edges are crunchy (give them a stir mid-way through the cooking to make sure they are not sticking).

Once done, cool, then mix with the peaches, making sure to include the peppers' cooking juices. Stir in the cumin, cayenne and lemon juice, plus a little more olive oil if you think it's necessary.

Pepper, cucumber and olive salad

 An attractive, great-tasting salad.

*1kg peppers of varying colours,
    cut into fine strips
1 cucumber, peeled, halved lengthways
    and then finely sliced
250g Kalamata olives (or any other variety),
    stoned if you can be bothered
50ml or more of Mustard Dressing
    (see page 75)
generous bunch of parsley, chopped
pinch cayenne pepper*

Mix all the ingredients and leave to marinate for 30 minutes or so before serving.

Spiro's lukewarm bean stew

 This recipe is in honour of Spiro the Shepherd whom I came across whilst lost on the slopes of Mount Pantecrator in the north of Corfu about 20 years ago. He insisted on inviting me back to his home where his wife had this bubbling on her stove. It is a bean dish that doesn't quite know if it is a salad or a soup: it all depends on the mood of the cook and how long it was left to simmer.

It should be slurpy, mealy and tomato-yummy – not at all like the tinned varieties. Best eaten tepid with distant views of the Albanian mountains – and the freshest possible bread to sop up the copious, delicious juices.

The main herb that the Corfiots are likely to use is rigani (see page 38), a wild relative of oregano that grows in profusion where goats having been grazing. Thus Spiro's wife would have told him to pick up some herbs on his way back from work. Your local supermarket in Corfu will stock it dried (look for a small, square, see-through plastic box); but whether you are trying this on holiday or at home, utilise any twiggy herb that you have got to hand: oregano or thyme will work just as well.

400g haricot or similar beans
50g tin tomato purée
1 mild onion, finely sliced
3 large cloves garlic, crushed
juice of 1 lemon
a few tbsps olive oil
water to cover
1 bay leaf
a couple of twigs of fresh rigani or oregano
salt and freshly ground black pepper
any fresh, chopped herb – parsley for
    preference – to serve

Heat a slick of oil in a suitable heavy-bottomed saucepan over a medium heat. Add the garlic, stir, and then add the tomato concentrate. Fry for five minutes and then add the beans. Fry for a further five minutes, stirring all the while, before adding the bay leaf, rigani and enough boiling water to cover the beans generously. Bring to a furious boil for 10 minutes (this helps to reduce the potent after-effects of the beans). Then turn the heat down to a gentle simmer, cover and leave to bubble, stirring regularly, for a good hour and half – start testing the beans for doneness after an hour and add more water if necessary. At the point you think the beans have got about another 20 minutes to go, add salt to taste (leaving the salt until towards the end of cooking helps prevent tough skins).

When the beans aren't quite ready to collapse, and the remaining sauce is thick and glossy, take off the heat and add the chopped onion, lemon juice and parsley to taste.

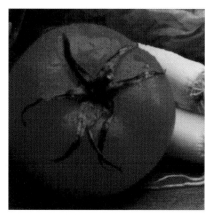

Sunburn salad

 So-named because the colours look similar to the bodies lined up on Ipsos Beach. The flavours are contrasting but pleasing together.

Per person:

80g watermelon per person, cut into
*   3cm cubes*
40g feta per person, cut into smaller cubes
handful of olives (optional)

Arrange in rows, rather than mixed together, and scatter olives (the melanomas!) over the top. Drizzle lightly with a simple olive-oil dressing, where the ratio of oil to lemon juice is 2:1

Tomato and red kidney bean salad

 A good way to perk up tomatoes that are not as flavoursome as they should be.

1 onion, diced
250ml tin red kidney beans, drained of liquid
4 large, or 6 medium, tomatoes,
*   roughly diced*
1 clove garlic, crushed
a few generous tbsps olive oil
10ml Greek wine vinegar
3 tbsp chopped parsley
1 tbsp tomato ketchup
salt and freshly ground black pepper

Soften the onion in a generous amount of olive oil, add the garlic and cook for a minute or so more. Add the ketchup and the beans, and cook for five minutes. Pop in a serving dish to cool slightly, then add the tomatoes, vinegar and parsley. Adjust seasoning and serve.

Main courses

Vasiliki's artichoke and broad bean stew

Vasiliki leads a busy life tending her olive trees, chickens and grandchildren, whilst providing domestic support for the Bennison household. Cooking is not in her job description – even if she had one – but she is an enthusiast and it is hard to keep her out of the kitchen. This is one of her recipes and is completely delicious: springtime on a plate.

You should choose artichokes no bigger than a golf ball, because at this size their choke (the hairy bit in the middle) has not developed, the stalk beneath the leaves is still tender enough to eat, and they don't need any extra preparation before being added to the stew. The rest of Vasiliki's recipe isn't constant, as the vegetable ratios vary according to availability. What she is not afraid to use, however, is a large amount of olive oil – newly pressed and from her own olive trees, of course.

1 kg very baby broad beans with the
  stalk end snapped off
18 tiny new potatoes – or fewer large
  ones, halved
18 baby artichokes
1 large onion, sliced
500ml water
300ml olive oil
2 heads fresh garlic, peeled and chopped
juice of up to 2 lemons
1 bunch fresh dill or fennel, chopped
half a tsp rigani (see page 38)
1 tsp each salt and freshly ground
  black pepper
small bunch chopped parsley and grated
képhalotyri cheese (see page 25) to serve

Heat the oil, and sauté the vegetables and herbs for a minute or so. Season, then add the water and at least a fruit's worth of lemon juice. Simmer gently until well and truly done. Let it cool slightly before checking to see if it needs more lemon juice. Stir in the parsley. If you plan to eat the vegetables hot, then grated cheese is quite a nice addition, but to my mind the cheese isn't necessary if you leave the stew until tepid before tucking in. If you can wait that long.

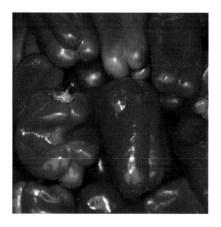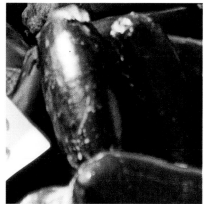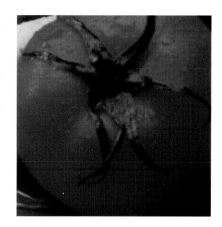

Aubergine layer terrine

This is an ideal dish for when you are entertaining, as it needs to be prepared the day before. Serve it with a lemony caper and tomato relish, and a green salad.

Oh, and I have cheated on occasion and used a couple of jars of grilled red peppers preserved in extra virgin olive oil (not vinegar) instead of grilling fresh ones.

3 large aubergines, cut into 1cm thick slices
12 large red peppers
200g feta cheese
100g manouri cheese (see page 25)
50ml olive oil
2 cloves garlic, crushed
3 tbsp shredded basil leaves
salt and freshly ground black pepper

For the relish:

450g tomatoes, cherry for preference, quartered
20 olives, stoned and chopped
200ml olive oil
juice and zest of 2 lemons
2 generous tbsp parsley, chopped
1 tbsp capers, rinsed
salt and freshly ground black pepper

Brush the aubergine slices with oil and dry-fry them until tender. You will need to do this in stages; when you have completed one batch, set the slices aside on a plate.

Meanwhile, grill the peppers until charred and then leave them in a resealable plastic bag to steam. When cool, remove the skin, stalks and seeds. Cut the peppers into large pieces and stir in the crushed garlic. Slice then crumble the cheeses together.

Put alternate layers of aubergines, peppers and cheese mixture in a 20-25cm springform cake tin. You can proceed in any order you like, but try to finish with aubergine, and sprinkle each layer with basil leaves, some freshly ground black pepper and a little salt. Press with a plate and a heavy weight, and chill overnight, placing the tin on a suitable plate or tray to catch any escaping juice. Finally, mix all the ingredients for the relish just before serving.

Bianco

In Italian, 'bianco' means that a dish has been made without tomatoes, so this classic Corfiot dish has Italian roots. For the fish, use either grey mullet or mackerel.

2kg fish, cleaned, with heads left on
    (see page 32)
4 large potatoes, peeled and sliced thickly
2 onions, finely sliced
500ml water
100ml olive oil
4 cloves of garlic crushed with a teaspoon
    of salt
juice of a lemon
pinch of rigani (see page 38)
1 bay leaf
salt and freshly ground pepper

In a large saucepan or casserole dish, sauté the onions until softened over a gentle heat. Add the garlic and potatoes and fry for a few minutes more. Then add the water and herbs, cover and simmer for 20 minutes, until the potatoes are nearly, but not quite, cooked. Place the fish on top of the potatoes so that they are semi-submerged in the cooking liquid – add more water if necessary. Replace the lid and simmer for another 15 minutes until the fish is done. Stir in the lemon juice and adjust the seasoning if necessary.

Bourthéto

Corfu's famous fish stew. The favoured base for this recipe is scorpion fish, but any fish can be used – the only proviso being that it is flavoursome enough not to be overpowered by the spicy fiery red sauce.

1.5-2kg fish, cleaned and gutted,
    heads still on (see page 32)
3 onions, finely diced
300ml water
150ml olive oil
5 cloves of garlic, crushed
3 tbsp tomato purée
2 tbsp chopped parsley
1 generous tbsp paprika
2 tsp cayenne pepper
    (more if you like things hot)
1 tsp salt

Preheat the oven to 180C / 350F / Gas 4. In a suitable ovenproof pan or casserole, sauté the onions in the oil until soft and golden. Then add the garlic, tomato purée and peppers, and fry for a minute or so, stirring all the time. Add the parsley and then the water; bring to a simmer and leave to bubble for 10 minutes. Add the whole fish to the pot, spooning over the tomato sauce so that they are all properly covered (you may need to add a little more water to achieve this, but the sauce shouldn't be too liquid). Bake for 35 minutes or so, depending on the size and shape of the fish.

Briam

Briam is basically a baked ratatouille with potatoes. In true Greek style, exact quantities are not important, but the order in which the veggies go into the baking pan or casserole is.

450g onions, peeled and sliced
450g potatoes, peeled and sliced
450g lime-yellow long peppers,
* deseeded and cut into strips*
450g ripe, decently flavoured
* tomatoes, sliced*
250g aubergines, thinly sliced
250g courgettes, sliced
200ml water
50ml olive oil
3 plump cloves of garlic, thinly slithered
bunch of parsley, chopped
salt and freshly ground black pepper

Preheat oven to 190C / 375F / Gas 5. Coat the bottom of a large casserole dish with a tablespoon of the oil, and layer the vegetables in the following order:

- half the onions
- potatoes
- peppers
- aubergine
- the rest of the onions
- courgettes
- tomatoes

As it goes in, sprinkle each layer with a little oil, some salt, pepper, garlic slithers and chopped parsley. Pour over the water, give a final season, then cover and bake for approximately one and half hours, checking occasionally to be sure it doesn't dry out before the vegetables are properly cooked (if it is, just add a little more water). Cool slightly before serving.

For a change of pace, crumble some feta over the top 20 minutes before the end of the cooking period. But remember to be sparing when seasoning the vegetables, as feta can be very salty.

All-in-one chicken roast

A Bennison-family, holiday-supper standard.

1 chicken, approx 2kg
4 large potatoes, washed and quartered
3 onions
100ml olive oil
1 glass white wine
several large twigs of rosemary
salt and freshly ground black pepper

Heat the oven to 200C / 400F / Gas 6. Peel the onions and trim the base – but not too severely, as you're going to quarter them, and you want the pieces to stay intact. Chuck the chicken, potatoes, onions and rosemary into a large roasting pan, and, using your hands, coat well with the olive oil. Pour over the white wine. Season, bake for one and a half hours, turning everything over half way through so that the meat and potatoes brown all over. Serve with a green salad.

Roast leg of kid with garlic and rosemary

Had enough of roasted lamb? Then try kid. If you have spotted the word 'kid' and are about to turn the page – don't! Kid is young goat; in this part of the world, it is both delicious and very similar to lamb in texture and flavour.

1.5-2kg leg of kid (or lamb)
350ml or so white wine
3 cloves garlic, peeled and slithered
sprig rosemary
salt and freshly ground black pepper

First preheat the oven to 200C / 400F / Gas 6. Then make 'plug-holes' in the meat by plunging the tip of a small sharp knife into the flesh and forcing a needle of rosemary and a slither of garlic into the cavity with a finger. Ideally, they should all disappear below the skin.

Season the joint generously with black pepper and salt. Place in a roasting tray with the white wine and roast for an hour or so (exactly how long depends on how pink or beige you like your meat; the Greeks roast their lamb until it is falling off the bone with exhaustion), basting occasionally with the wine and juices.

A final note. You could be very un-Greek and also add anchovies to the plug-holes before roasting. Blame the French for inventing this habit. Lots of people go 'yeuch' at anchovies, but you won't be able to taste them, promise. The flavours meld to create something absolutely ambrosial. Call me dull and boring, but I now don't do lamb or kid any other way – unless I have forgotten to stock up on the anchovies.

Leeks with rice

This has been a favourite supper dish of mine for as long as I can remember, which I grew up calling Leeks à la Grecque – probably because of the generous amounts of olive oil, olives and lemon juice that are used.

Measuring rice by volume is more useful than weighing, as it helps when judging how much water you will need: as a rule of thumb, use double the amount of water to the volume of rice.

4 large leeks, trimmed and sliced into
* 1cm rounds*
20 or so olives
600ml boiling water
300ml long-grain rice
150ml olive oil
juice of 1 lemon
2 tbsp tomato purée
2 tsp salt, several generous grinds of
* black pepper*
parsley, chopped

Soften the leeks in the olive oil over a low heat, which should take about 10 minutes. Then add the rice and stir until the grains are well mixed with the leeks and thoroughly coated with oil. Stir in the tomato purée, season and add the boiling water, stirring all the time. Cover and leave to simmer gently for 10 minutes. Now check how much water has been absorbed: there should be some liquid left. If not, add 50ml or so more boiling water and stir. Then replace the lid, turn off the heat and leave for 10 minutes.

Finally, add the lemon juice, stir through the parsley and scatter the olives over the top. Serve with chunks of fresh crusty bread and butter.

Vasiliki's meatballs

Another of Vasiliki's delicious recipes, these are excellent with a tomato sauce (see page 75) and pasta. Alternatively, squash the meatballs into patties and grill on the barbeque, before serving hot in pitta bread with a little crumbled feta, mint and shredded lettuce.

1.5kg ground beef
1 onion, finely chopped or grated
3 slices two-day-old bread, cubed
1 egg, beaten
2 tbsp chopped parsley
1 tsp rigani (see page 38)
1 tsp salt
olive oil
freshly ground black pepper

First preheat the oven to 200C / 400F / Gas 6. While it's heating, soak the bread cubes in a little water for a couple of minutes, drain and then squeeze out the excess. Now add the bread and all the remaining ingredients to the beef, and mix together very thoroughly. Make little golfball-sized nuggets of the mixture and place them on an oiled baking tray. Dribble a little oil over the meatballs, then bake for 30 minutes or fry until brown on all sides.

Moussaka

Bad moussaka is easy to find: reheated, dried out but still leaking oil like a beached tanker. It might be one of Greece's national dishes, but it probably originated on the eastern side of the country and most certainly did not come from Corfu, where the seasoning is lighter and the aubergine is considered an important component of the dish.

Most recipes tell you to salt aubergines first 'to rid them of bitter juices'; well, I suspect that these days aubergines are bred not to have bitter juices because I have never bothered to salt them and, so far, none of them have tasted nasty. But their tendency to absorb oil when they are fried, only to release it all during the baking process, is more of a problem. To avoid this, brush each slice with oil and then dry-fry, grill or bake them.

Minced beef is now the meat most often used in moussaka. Buy 'ground beef' rather than 'mince', as the latter will be far fattier.

1-1.5kg aubergines cut into 1cm slices
1kg flavourful ripe tomatoes or 2 boxes
    of sieved tomatoes
500g ground beef
1 large onion, finely diced
100ml red wine
1 garlic clove, crushed
4 tbsp chopped parsley
2 tbsp olive oil, plus extra for
    brushing aubergine
1 bay leaf
half a tsp cinnamon

For the béchamel sauce:

575ml warm milk
3 egg yolks
55g or 2 tbsp flour
55g butter
50g képhalotyri cheese (see page 25)
1 bay leaf
several scrapes of nutmeg
salt and freshly ground pepper

Dry fry the aubergine slices until golden (see left). Then make the meat sauce: sauté the onions until soft, then add the garlic before turning up the heat. Add the beef and cook until browned, then add the tomatoes, wine, cinnamon and bay leaf. Season with salt and pepper, before leaving the sauce to simmer for an hour or so, toppping up with a little water if the pan shows signs of drying out before the meat is tender, and stirring in the parsley right at the end.

Meanwhile, make the béchamel sauce. Melt the butter over a low heat, and stir in the flour to make a roux, cooking it gently for three or four minutes. Now gradually add the milk to the roux, beating all the time. Once all the milk is in, add the bay leaf and nutmeg, and simmer for 15 minutes or so, stirring occasionally. Remove the bay leaf before beating in the egg yolks followed by half the cheese. Season, and stir two tablespoons of the resulting béchamel into the meat sauce.

Next, take a deep baking pan and use half the aubergine slices to make a slightly overlapping layer at the bottom. Add the meat sauce, and then cover with the rest of the aubergines. Pour over the béchamel sauce, sprinkle with the rest of the grated cheese and bake at 180C / 350F / Gas 4 for an hour or so.

Psarósoupa (fish soup)

Psarósoupa occasionally makes an appearance on taverna menus. I was alerted to it by my godchildren (aged nine and 11), who are regular visitors to Corfu and think that Greek fish stew is better than Spanish. So there.

1.5kg fish, cleaned, gutted and left on the bone (see page 32). Use a mixture of types, such as red and grey mullet

500g tomatoes, chopped
   (or a tin if the fresh ones are lacking in flavour)

2 onions, diced

2 carrots, grated

2 courgettes, diced

1 leek, sliced into thin circles

500ml water

120ml olive oil

4 cloves garlic, crushed

juice of a lemon

bunch sélino (see page 38), chopped
   (or a couple of celery sticks with leaves, chopped, if no sélino is available)

2 bay leaves

1 strip lemon peel

1 tsp each cayenne pepper and salt

bunch parsley, chopped, to serve

The aim is to make a flavoursome, chunky vegetable stew, before adding the fish about 10-15 minutes before you want to eat.

Soften the onions and leek in the olive oil over a gentle heat; they should go mushy but not colour. Add the garlic and soften for a couple more minutes, before mixing in the tomatoes, courgettes, carrots, sélino, bay leaves, cayenne pepper and salt. Give everything a good stir, cover, and leave to simmer for 5 minutes.

Now add the lemon peel, lemon juice and water. Cover again and leave for another 20 minutes.

Whilst the vegetables are cooking, cut the fish into chunks across the bone. Don't discard the heads – they will add lots of flavour to the soup. How long the fish chunks need to cook for depends on the type of fish and the size you have cut them up into. But they will cook quite quickly, so keep an eye on them after the first 5 minutes of simmering. The odd flake or two coming adrift is okay but you don't want a mush. Once the fish is just done, add the parsley, adjust the seasoning, and serve. The Greeks think the best flesh comes from the heads; if you agree, leave them in the serving dish.

Pastitsatha

Pastitsatha, or beef and pasta casserole, is a Corfiot speciality. The addition of pasta to the sauce is a way of making meat go further and generating two courses out of a one-pot dish (the meat is removed after cooking and either served on the side or as a separate course). I omit the traditional wine vinegar – the flavour can be too dominating sometimes.

Incidentaly, you may also find versions of this dish using jointed cockeral instesd of beef.

1.5 kg beef (stewing steak is fine)
    cut into large chunks –
    about cigarette-packet size
500g uncooked weight macaroni
2 large onions, finely chopped or whizzed in
    a food processor
250ml of olive oil
250 ml red wine
4 or 5 cloves garlic, crushed
3 bay leaves
1 tbsp wine vinegar
2 tbsp of tomato purée
1 tbsp cayenne pepper (optional)
1 tsp of cinnamon – or a cinnamon stick
1 tsp paprika
half a tsp cloves
salt and freshly ground black pepper
plenty of grated parmesan to serve

Heat the oil over a medium heat, brown the beef in it two or three pieces at a time, and then add the onion. Stir and let fry for a minute before adding the spices. Then add the garlic. Stir once more and pour over the red wine and vinegar. Give the pan bottom a good scrape to incorporate all the flavourful caramelised bits and then add the tomato purée. Simmer with the lid on for about one and a half hours, topping up with water to make sure you end up with an abundance of nice thick sauce that covers the meat. When the meat is tender, remove, cover and keep warm – don't let it dry out.

Boil the macaroni for the time on the packet, less 5 minutes. Drain and add the pasta to the sauce. Stir continuously until the pasta has finished cooking, and serve sprinkle with the grated parmesan.

Pork with quince

 A dish for autumn, when the heavenly quince makes its appearance in the market. If you are not familiar with it, look for a fruit that resembles a large misshapen yellow pear – possibly covered with grey fluff – and sniff: if you have got hold of the right thing, the warmly aromatic odour will have your nostrils flaring with pleasure.

This recipe is inspired by a meal I had in Corfu Town one October. But it is only an approximation, as my Greek was for once better than the waiters' English, so we weren't able to discuss the quantities involved.

1.5 kg pork meat – shoulder or leg –
*   cut into 3cm cubes*
2 large onions, either finely chopped
*   or whizzed in a food processor*
2 large quinces, peeled, cored, and
*   cut into 2cm chunks*
2 glasses white wine (plus one for the cook)
5 tbsp olive oil
1 clove of garlic, crushed
juice and zest of half a lemon
1 bay leaf
1 tsp sugar or more to taste
half a tsp each of ground cinnamon
*   and cloves*
salt and freshly ground black pepper

Preheat the oven to 180C / 350F / Gas 4. To achieve a nice tan on the pork, you will probably have to sauté the cubes in batches, to stop the meat from steaming. So, in a heavy-bottomed ovenproof pan with a lid, heat the oil, add five to six pieces of pork, and fry until brown on all sides. Remove and repeat until done.

Add the onion and more oil if necessary. Fry gently – you are aiming for softened onion, but the meat juices might make it stick, so keep giving the pan a good stir.

Add the salt and spices, stir, and add the pork. Pour in the wine, scrape up all the caramelised juices at the bottom of the pan, and stir a bit more. Chuck in the bay leaf and be generous with the pepper mill.

Now add enough water to cover the meat, cover and pop into the oven for an hour, after which you should add the quince, lemon zest and juice, and sugar, plus more water if necessary. Replace in the oven for another 45 minutes or so. Serve with mashed potatoes or pasta, and don't be alarmed by the very pretty pink colour of the sauce.

Sweet potato and Greek cheese bake

Corfiots are very fond of sweet potatoes, which make their appearance in the autumn. This supper dish is good for when the October storms arrive and mounds of sweet potatoes are everywhere in the shops.

3 large sweet potatoes
3 large firm, red skinned potatoes or
*   any other variety suitable for baking*
2 red onions
2 red peppers
2 yellow peppers
8 cloves garlic
50g each of halloumi and manouri cheese
*   (see page 25), sliced as thinly as possible*
4 tbsp olive oil
freshly ground black pepper

Preheat the oven to 200C / 400F / Gas 6. Peel both types of potato, then cut the sweet potatoes into rough 4cm cubes and the red potatoes into smaller 2.5cm ones, as the sweet potato will cook more quickly. Peel, halve and quarter the red onions. De-seed the peppers and cut into 2.5cm squares. Separate and peel the cloves of garlic.

Put everything except the cheeses into a roasting tin big enough to accommodate the vegetables easily – or use two tins, as if the veggies are too closely packed they will steam rather than roast. Give everything a good coating of olive oil, and season with the black pepper (not salt, as the halloumi is already salty enough). Cook for 45 minutes or until the vegetables are cooked through and tinged with brown.

Now turn the oven up to maximum. Place the cheeses on top of the vegetables and replace the dish either in the very hot oven, or under a grill. Let the cheese melt and begin to brown – about five to 10 minutes. Serve immediately with a green salad.

Sofrito

Sofrito, or beef stewed with garlic and parsley, is one of Corfu's classic dishes. Traditionally this recipe called for vinegar alone to be used in making the stew, but quite a few Corfiots these days think wine gives a nicer flavour. And a Greek friend once suggested that the only reason cooks in the past used vinegar was to hide the taste of an iffy bit of meat.

1.5kg rump steak, sliced 2cms thick
350ml dry white wine
100ml olive oil
2 tbsp decent wine vinegar (optional)
1 head garlic, cloves peeled and crushed
*   into a paste with salt*
1 large bunch of parsley, chopped
1 twig of mint, chopped
seasoned flour for dusting
freshly ground black pepper

Cover each slice of beef with cling film, bash them until very thin with a rolling pin, then roll each slice up – the result should be rolls about 1cm thick. Dust both sides of the rolls with flour and pat off the excess.

Using a heavy-bottomed frying pan, brown the beef in batches in the oil. Now mix the garlic paste with the parsley and mint. Put a layer of browned beef at the bottom of a casserole, and scatter with a good grind of black pepper and a spoonful of the garlic mixture; continue until all the meat is used up. Add the wine and vinegar; if the meat isn't completely submerged, add water until it is. Simmer gently for an hour or so, until the meat is very tender and the sauce thick.

Min's mother-in-law's squid in red sauce, with pasta

Min is one of the many hundreds of British women who went off to Corfu to work, but then met and married a handsome, wonderful Greek – called Apostoli, in Min's case – never to return to the UK. This recipe was given to her by her mother-in-law, who wanted to make sure her beloved son was fed properly.

1kg squid, cut into medium-sized pieces
    (see page 32)
enough thin spaghetti for six people
1 onion, grated
50ml olive oil
2 and a half tbsp tomato purée
2 and a half tsp of sea salt crystals
half a tsp ground black pepper
grated képhalotyri cheese (see page 25)
    for serving

Put all the ingredients except the spaghetti and cheese in a saucepan, and pour over enough water to cover them by about 4cms. Bring to a simmer, then cover and cook slowly for approximately one and a half hours, or until the kalamari are tender and the sauce is thick.

In another pan, boil the spaghetti according to the manufacturer's instructions. Mix the pasta and sauce together and serve with the grated képhalotyri on the side.

Two of Apostoli and Min's children don't like kalamari cooked this way; they prefer it fried. If you are faced with a similar situation, make the sauce without adding the kalamari, perhaps adding a small amount of chopped sélino (see page 38). Prepare the kalamari sacs into flat squares as described on page 32, then fry in olive oil over a medium heat for 30 seconds on each side. Squeeze lemon juice over the pieces when cooked and serve on top of the tomato pasta.

Stifado

Traditionally the meat used is rabbit – but the recipe here is a 'city' version as beef is easier to come by. The baby onions are a key feature: 'Where were they?' Greek friends once asked, when I had run out of time and served up a sort of French daube that used sliced ordinary onions instead.

1.5kg beef stewing steak, cut into cigarette-
    packet-sized pieces
1kg small onions or shallots, peeled and
    left whole
400g good-flavoured plum tomatoes,
    chopped and juices retained (if the
    tomatoes are tasteless, use passata)
150ml red wine
50ml olive oil
3 large cloves of garlic, crushed
2 tbsp Greek red wine vinegar
4 tbsp parsley, chopped
3 bay leaves
8cm stick of cinnamon broken into 3 pieces
several scrapes of nutmeg
salt and freshly ground black pepper

Preheat the oven to 170C / 325F / Gas 3. Heat the oil in a large pan, then brown the meat, followed by the onions. Pour in the wine and vinegar, and stir, scraping up and dissolving the caramelised bits before adding the bay leaves, cinnamon, tomatoes and garlic. If the meat is not covered with liquid, then top up with water, season and cover, ensuring a tight seal by putting a sheet of aluminium foil between the pan and its lid. Cook for two hours or so, checking occasionally and removing the lid towards the end if the sauce needs to reduce more. Stir in the parsley and serve with mashed potatoes or pasta.

Stuffed squid

Use larger squid for this dish – it is less of a fiddle if you do. This recipe uses three pans – one more than I like on holiday, but luckily cooks don't wash up in my household.

1.5kg squid, cleaned, bodies intact, tentacles
    chopped up (see page 32)
3 ripe tomatoes, chopped
2 onions, finely diced
500ml dry white wine
150g long grain rice
150ml olive oil
50g pine nuts
1 tbsp each of parsley and mint,
    chopped together
half a tsp rigani (see page 38)
salt and freshly ground black pepper

Heat half the oil in a fry pan and soften the onions, then add the squid tentacles, pine nuts, rice and herbs. Season – be generous with the pepper – and sauté for a further couple of minutes. Remove from the heat.

In another pan, heat the remaining oil and fry the squid bodies briefly, so that they stiffen. (This makes them easier to stuff.) Half-fill each with the rice mixture and pour a little of the wine over the mixture before folding the tops shut. Pack the squid in pairs with the folded ends pressed together in a suitable casserole.

Add the chopped tomatoes, remaining wine and a pinch of salt to the pan you used to fry the squid. Heat and pour it carefully over the squid, before covering and cooking in a moderate oven 180C / 350F / Gas 4 for an hour. You may need to add water towards the end, but you are aiming for a sauce that has succeeded in helping the rice to cook, so it is not a disaster if there's a small amount left over.

In the Greek manner, leave it to cool a little before serving.

Barbeques

Often the preference on holiday is to slave over hot coals rather than a hot oven. Preparation and protection from the brisk westerly evening wind (a common feature of Corfu) are the keys to success. Keep your mind open about cooking times, too: the variables of wind speed, ambient temperature, and type of charcoal will all affect how long you have to wait before dinner is ready.

Getting the fire going

Actually the last thing you want are flames to cook over: you should be aiming for red-hot coals that in daylight look dusty. So start the fire well before you want to cook; allow at least 30 minutes for the flames subside and the coals to collapse into a bed about 5cm deep. Ultra, ultra-hot coals are only useful for grilling steaks; if you are planning to grill anything else, wait until the coals are slightly cooler.

Approximate rules of thumb:

- If you have to snatch your hand away immediately you try putting it about 10cms above the coals, you're at steak temperature

- If you can keep your hand in the vicinity for three or four seconds, you have a grilling-chicken temperature

Other things to bear in mind:

- Start with a clean barbeque. In other words, don't be tempted to think the gunk will burn off. Clear out all the old ashes and use a wire bush to scrub off charcoaled food particles

- Do not use petrol-based lighters to start the fire – the taste can taint the food

- If you are going to use wood, avoid pine or any other conifer wood – unless you want your food to taste like retsina

Grilling meat

The most common way of eating grilled meat in Greece is *souvlakia*, or kebabs. *Souvlakia* comes from the Greek word *souvla*, meaning any kind of skewer or spit. Here are some pointers for doing your own.

Barbequed meat benefits from a marinade, as the oil helps to keep the meat from drying out. A marinade also improves flavour but it is no miracle cure for tough cuts of meat – these should be stewed. For an easy marinade, whisk together approximately equal quantities of olive oil and lemon juice with *rigani* (see page 38) for flavouring. Do not be tempted to use vinegar instead of lemon – the result isn't nearly as good. Pour into a dish that can hold the kebabs flat. Leave for at least an hour before cooking, turning the skewers every so often. If using bamboo skewers, soak them in water first as this stops them from burning.

Pork should be cooked further from the coals – and for longer – than lamb or beef to ensure that is cooked through. To help prevent the meat from sticking, oil the rack first, and don't poke or fiddle with the meat for the first couple of minutes – that way you will allow to form a crisp surface.

Dripping fat sometimes creates flames, which you don't want. So keep a bowl of water next to the barbeque and sprinkle water onto the flames to dampen them down. But don't be too liberal, or you'll extinguish the lot.

Grilling fish

Cooking fish over a barbeque is quite tricky because it is terribly easy to overdo them. The ideal weight range for grilling is 450, and 650g-450g is about the right amount for one person. However, fish aren't always that obliging about their shape or weight.

Eat your fish on the day of purchase. Pop them, cleaned, into a marinade and keep in the fridge until about 15-20 minutes before you intend to barbeque them (letting the fish come to room temperature first helps the flesh to cook evenly).

Set the grill about 12cms above the coals. As with meat, oil the fish and the grill beforehand and then don't be tempted to fiddle as they cook. A double sided, hinged grill is ideal as it stops the chef from interfering, whilst allowing him (or her, but barbequing always seems to be a bloke's thing) to turn them over.

If one of these is not to hand, turn the fish over by sliding a spatula under it from the tail up the body. Do not turn the fish over via its tummy, as this will increase the chances of bits breaking off.

Slashing a fish two or three times across the body helps it to cook quicker and to judge when the flesh is cooked. A 450g sea bass, for example, should be ready after six to eight minutes grilling on each side.

Grilling vegetables

If your attempts with mixed vegetable *souvlakia* result in tomato sludge and rock-hard but burnt baby onions, try keeping to one kind of vegetable per skewer. The radical alternative is: don't use skewers. The first thing one does once they're cooked is burn your fingers un-impaling the veggies, so life is much easier if you dispense with this step altogether.

Grilled veggies also make a wonderful salad: the trick is to slosh on the oil and lemon juice after cooking.

Peppers Grill them whole, turning frequently until the skin is charred. Pop them into a bowl and cover with cling film to cool, by which time the skins are easy to peel off. De-stalk, de-seed, and cut into the shape you want

Onions Need long cooking and regular basting with oil. Cut each one into quarters first, keeping the root base attached so that it doesn't fall apart

Aubergines Slice lengthwise and grill without oil until soft and toasted

Courgettes Slice lengthwise (and then in half, if they are large) into four pieces. Grill without oil

Mushrooms Remove the stems. Grill without oil, cap-side down first. When you see moisture appearing from the stem-space, turn them gill-side down for one minute

Tomatoes Grill whole

Sauces and dressings

Avgolémono sauce

This very useful egg and lemon mixture is used to thicken and flavour soups, as well as the cooking juices from wide variety of dishes. For example, instead of plain boiled green beans, follow this recipe and use some of the water in which they were boiled to make this sauce.

4 egg yolks
4 tbsps lemon juice
2 tbsps or so of hot stock from the dish you
    are going to thicken

Beat the egg yolks until light. Whilst you continue to beat, slowly add the lemon juice, followed by the hot, but not boiling, stock. Stir this mixture into the pot that contains the rest of the stock or juices and above all do not let it boil.

Cheat's avgolémono sauce

The slight problem with real avgolemono sauce is that is prone to curdling. So here is a cheat's version where you make a flour-based sauce with the stock.

250ml of hot stock / liquid
2 eggs, beaten
juice of 2 lemons
1 tbsp flour
1 tbsp melted butter

Warm the melted butter in a non-stick saucepan. Add the flour and stir vigorously with a wooden spoon for a minute or so. Gradually add the hot stock, a spoonful at a time to begin with, into the butter/flour mixture. Make sure the stock is properly incorporated before adding any more liquid. In another bowl, beat the eggs until light and fluffy. Gradually add the lemon juice, beating all the while. Now add the hot – but not boiling – sauce to the egg mixture. Return to a gentle heat and stir for a few moments.

Mustard dressing

I find that recipes for salad dressing specify a ratio of olive oil to vinegar that ranges from 1:1 to about 4:1. To my mind, the latter is okay with lemon juice, but way too sharp if using ordinary vinegar. You may disagree, so do adjust the amount of vinegar (the Greek, red-wine type that comes in plastic see-through bottles) accordingly.

8 tbsp olive oil
1 tbsp vinegar
1 heaped tsp Dijon mustard
   (or 1 level tsp mustard powder)
1 clove garlic, crushed
half a tsp sugar
pinch salt

Start by mixing the mustard, garlic, sugar and salt. If you don't want your vinaigrette to separate, whisk in the vinegar and then the oil last of all – this will help make it pleasantly thick and glossy-looking.

Tomato sauce no 1:
baked tomato and olive sauce

This recipe is slightly more hassle than some others for tomato sauce, but sometimes the tomatoes available need more oomph, and baking them first gives the sauce more depth of flavour. It's particularly good with pasta or with the aubergine layer terrine on page 61.

1.5kg tomatoes, halved
250g olives, rinsed, stoned and chopped
2 large onions, diced very small
5 cloves of garlic, finely chopped
olive oil
a pinch each of cayenne pepper,
   salt and sugar

Put the tomatoes, cut-side up, in a roasting tin, packing them in quite tightly so they don't fall over and spill their juices during cooking. Sprinkle with the garlic, cayenne, salt and sugar, then lightly drizzle with olive oil. Bake for 40 minutes, checking towards the end that they are not burning.

While the tomatoes are in the oven, gently stew the onions in a couple of tablespoons or so of olive oil until they are soft. Once they are ready, and the tomatoes have cooled, purée the lot together and then sieve the mixture to remove the tomato skins. Finally, stir in the olives before serving.

Tomato sauce no 2:
easy tomato sauce

A sauce that requires minimal effort and is great with pasta or meatballs.

250ml tin sieved tomatoes
150ml red wine.
4 tbsp olive oil
1 clove of garlic, crushed
1 bay leaf
salt and freshly ground black pepper

Put all the ingredients into a saucepan, place on a gentle to moderate heat, stir and cover. Leave for 30 minutes. Adjust the seasoning and serve.

Skorthaliá

This is a tremendously popular sauce in Greece, most often served with grilled fresh fish, or salt cod boiled with potatoes. Locals might think it heresy, but I also like it with hard-boiled eggs. Sometimes *skorthaliá* is made with potatoes, but this version uses bread and ground almonds instead. So if you have a food processor, great, but if not then you will get a workout from using a wooden spoon to pound everything to an emulsion.

For about 300ml sauce:

6cm cubes of stale white bread,
crusts removed
125ml olive oil
100g ground almonds
(ideally grind blanched almonds yourself
to give a crunchier texture)
4 or more cloves of garlic, crushed with a
small amount of salt
Greek wine vinegar to taste
a little water

Soak the bread in a very small amount of water for a few minutes, then squeeze it all out so that you are left with a paste. Stir in the ground almonds and the garlic so that everything is thoroughly incorporated. Then add the oil as if you were making mayonnaise: start by just adding a drop of oil at a time, beating all the while. Keep adding oil, gradually in creasing the amounts, until the mixture turns shiny – at this point the bread and almond mixture cannot absorb any more oil. Taste, and sharpen with a few drops of vinegar if necessary.

Sweet things

Baclavá

Baclavá are nut-filled filo pastries, soaked in syrup. They look so complicated you might imagine they are impossible to make in a domestic kitchen, but actually it is a fairly straightforward exercise, and well-worth doing if you find the commercially made versions too sweet.

For 12 portions:

12 sheets filo pastry (unthawed, if frozen)
250g clarified butter (see page 24)
100g chopped walnuts
100g chopped hazelnuts
100g chopped almonds
90g sugar
1 tbsp ground cinnamon
half a tsp ground cloves
several scrapes of nutmeg

For the syrup:

250g castor sugar
juice and zest of a lemon
juice and zest of an orange
5cm stick of cinnamon
2 tbsp water

Separate the sheets of filo pastry into four piles – two piles of four sheets, and two piles of two sheets – and cover with a clean, damp cloth. Oil a baking tin with some butter (choose a deep tin, around 5cm smaller than the filo sheets are wide); in a separate bowl, mix together the nuts, spices and sugar.

Now take the first four sheets of pastry, and one by one lay them flat in the tin, brushing each layer with the clarified butter. Cover with a third of the nut mixture, then add the next two sheets of pastry, again brushing each one with butter. Add another third of the nut mixture, two more sheets of filo brushed with butter, and the final third of the nuts. Top with the last four sheets of butter-brushed filo and tuck the edges in neatly. Using a sharp knife, divide into 12 pieces (diamond or rectangular, whichever your artistic preference) and bake for approximately 45 minutes or until golden.

Shortly before the baclavá is ready, dissolve all the ingredients for the syrup in a small pan, and simmer for around five minutes. Take the baclavá from the oven, the syrup from the stove, and pour over the pastry. Leave to cool until edible and eat straight away – immediate consumption may not be traditional, but is a wonderful indulgence.

Bobóta

Baking cakes on holiday? Well this is a traditional cake, a bit like a crumbly, nutty fruitcake, found throughout the Ionian Islands – and it doesn't require strictly accurate measurement of ingredients, temperature or time spent in the oven. So the most challenging part of the whole business will be finding a suitable mixing bowl.

1kg fine cornmeal
200g whole almonds, toasted then
  bashed into largish bits
250ml orange juice
250ml olive oil
100g honey
  (if solid, dissolve in a little hot water)
100g sultanas or currants
100g walnuts halves, bashed quite small
2 tbsp orange rind, grated
1 sachet or 2 heaped tsp baking powder
1 heaped tsp ground cinnamon
1 tsp ground cloves

Stir the dry ingredients together, and then add the liquids, mixing to form a stiff dough (add more water or orange juice if necessary). You'll have enough to fill a 30cm diameter, 6cm deep pie tin – oil it, press in the dough, and bake for about 50 minutes. Good eaten with a cup of Earl Grey tea.

Creamed apricots

An excellent way of making stewed apricots go a little further, which I came up with one night when friends unexpectedly stayed for dinner. It's very straightforward: just don't let wine and good company make you forget about the fruit simmering away merrily on the stove.

500g dried apricots
250ml double cream, whipped until it
  just holds its peaks
125g sugar, or more to taste
125g cup ground almonds
2 tbsp apricot brandy (optional)

Ideally, soak the apricots for several hours before stewing them. Drain, put in a pan, cover with more water, and simmer until they are soft – aim for a gooey sludge that isn't burnt round the edges. You might need to add extra water at intervals, and should keep stirring the mix towards the end of the cooking time, otherwise the apricots will stick. Once cooked, add the sugar and almonds and mix well. Let the mixture cool before folding in the cream and the brandy if using. Divide equally between six wine glasses and chill.

Watermelon Crush

A sort of granita. Find yourself a nice watermelon. Open it up, remove the black pips and scoop out the flesh – how much depends on how many you are catering for – and mash it up a bit. Do this in a bowl so the juice doesn't go everwhere. Bung it all in an ice tray or zipper plastic bag and put it in the freezer for 30 minutes or so until the melon has started to crystallise but hasn't turned solid. Decant into wine glasses.

For a variation on the theme, add some vodka or freshly squeezed orange juice prior to freezing.

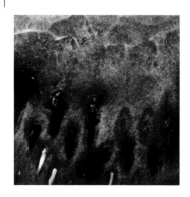

Yiayiá's pelargonium-scented yoghurt cake

 Lining a cake tin with small, scented pelargonium leaves infuses its contents with a wonderful perfume. (For the non-gardeners amongst you, pelargonium is the correct name for geraniums, though the right varieties for this recipe are not those found trailing from window boxes. You are interested instead in the plants which are upright in their growing habit, with tiny pale flowers and tough, feathery leaves.) The habit came from a *yiayiá* – the Greek word for granny – who lived in Porta, a village on the slopes of Mt Pantecrator. Her recipe is of the '2 scoops flour, 1 pot yoghurt' variety, so I have turned these rough-and-ready measurements into grams.

450g flour
225g soft butter
225g sugar
225g yoghurt
4 eggs, separated
a handful of skinned, chopped almonds
2 level tsp baking powder
half a level tsp bicarbonate of soda
half a tsp vanilla extract
pinch of salt

Preheat the oven to 180C / 350F / Gas 4. Grease a cake tin, and put three or four rose- or orange- scented pelargonium leaves on the base. Sieve together the flour, baking powder and bicarbonate of soda. Beat the butter very well and, still beating, gradually add the sugar followed by the vanilla extract. Then add the egg yolks one by one, beating each one in thoroughly before adding the next, and continuing to until the mixture is shiny – about three minutes or so. Stir in the yoghurt, followed by the flour mixture.

Whisk the egg whites to stiff peaks, then fold gently into the mixture with a metal spoon. Put into the cake tin and sprinkle the almonds on top. Bake for 45 minutes or until a metal skewer pushed into the middle of the cake comes out clean.

If you cannot find pelargonium leaves, try the following instead. While the cake is cooking, simmer 300g castor sugar, 400ml water and one thinly sliced lemon for 15 minutes to make a light syrup. Pour over the cake when it has cooled.

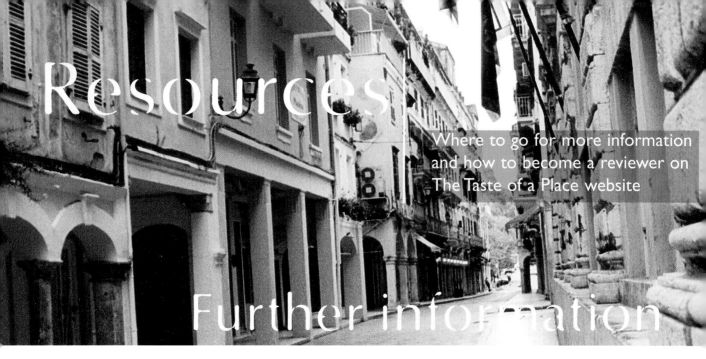

Resources

Further information

If this book has whetted your appetite for knowledge as well as Greek cuisine, there are some other sources of information you may want to explore.

Books

For an insight into food culture and the historical development of Corfiot cooking, try 'Prospero's Kitchen' by Diana Farr Louis and June Marinos. This excellent book is published in paperback by Pedestrian Publications in Corfu and is available in bookshops around the island. Or look out for second-hand copies of 'A Kitchen in Corfu' by James Chatto and Wendy Martin (Weidenfeld and Nicolson, 1987), now sadly out of print. Alan Davidson's 'Mediterranean Seafood' (Prospect Books, new edition out in June 2002) is also very useful if you are interested in learning more about locally available fish.

An indispensable help when buying local wines is 'An Illustrated Guide to Greek Wines' by Nico Manessis (Olive Press Publications). It is not that easy to find copies, so place your order at one of the bookshops in Corfu Town at the beginning of your holiday.

UK-based websites

Anyone who wants to continue cooking these recipes once back home will find that many Greek ingredients are readily available in the supermarkets. But as the essence of Corfiot cooking is to use the best possible fresh local produce, you should consider sourcing your ingredients with a little help from the following websites, all of which have extensive links to other useful organisations.

www.farmersmarkets.net
provides information on farmer's markets around Britain

www.wimarkets.co.uk
lists all the Women's Institute markets around the UK

www.fooduk.com
is a portal devoted to specialist British food producers

www.bigbarn.co.uk
locates fresh produce in the area where you live

www.mcsuk.org
is the website of the Marine Conservation Society; visit it to find out which fish species are under threat, or to order their Good Fish Guide

Greek wine

Of the UK high-street chains, Oddbins stocks the best range of Greek wines. Get hold of their catalogue, or visit their website at **www.oddbins.co.uk**. The website **www.greekwines.gr** is devoted to Greek wine, and also provides links to the sites of individual winemakers.

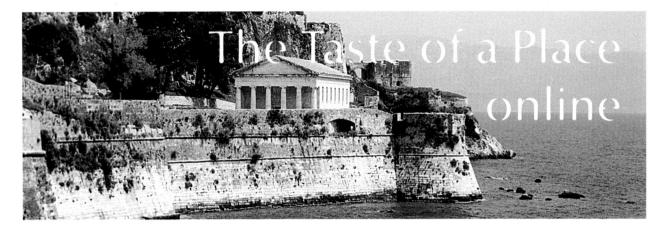

The Taste of a Place online

The Taste of a Place isn't just a book. It's also an online resource, where you can log on to find out which tavernas are recommended – both by us and by readers – in the area you are interested in. So we need your help.

Take a look at the printed form overleaf. If you discover a Corfiot taverna that you think is worthy of recommendation, either photocopy the form, fill it in and send it to us at Wittersham Publishing, PO Box 39705 London, W4 4WA, or log on to **www.the-taste-of-a-place.com** and submit your review online.

Getting online on holiday

If you want to nominate a taverna or read current reviews while in Corfu, you will need local access to the net. Be warned that if you have bought your laptop with you expecting to plug into the telephone network that a) the sockets differ and b) the local telephone exchange may be about 40 years old – particularly in rural areas. It is much simpler and better for your blood pressure to find an internet café.

All the main resorts have at least one such café, and you should find that your local friendly travel agent also offers access to the internet. Charges vary, with the minimum of 15 or 20 minutes costing from one and a half euros upwards. Out of the Blue in Kassiopi remains open all year, while the biggest and most central internet café in Corfu Town is at 28 Kapidistra, opposite the Spianada.

While you're online, check out the Friends of the Ionian's useful website, which covers food, wine, environmental and cultural issues. It can be found at **www.foi.org.uk**

Taverna Review

1. Name of establishment ....

2. Name of village ....

3. Whereabouts in village ....

Please tick the following:

A Location		B Food		C Service		D Good for children		E Good for grown-ups	
Horrible	1	Horrible	1	Horrible	1	Horrible	1	Horrible	1
Tolerable	2	Tolerable	2	Tolerable	2	Tolerable	2	Tolerable	2
Good	3	Good	3	Good	3	Good	3	Good	3
Brilliant	4	Brilliant	4	Brilliant	4	Brilliant	4	Brilliant	4

Any memorable or unusual dishes? ....
....

Any other comments (max 50 words) ....
....
....
....

When you visited: ....

How can we contact you? (Your name, address and email if appropriate)
....
....
....
....

the taste of a place
corfu

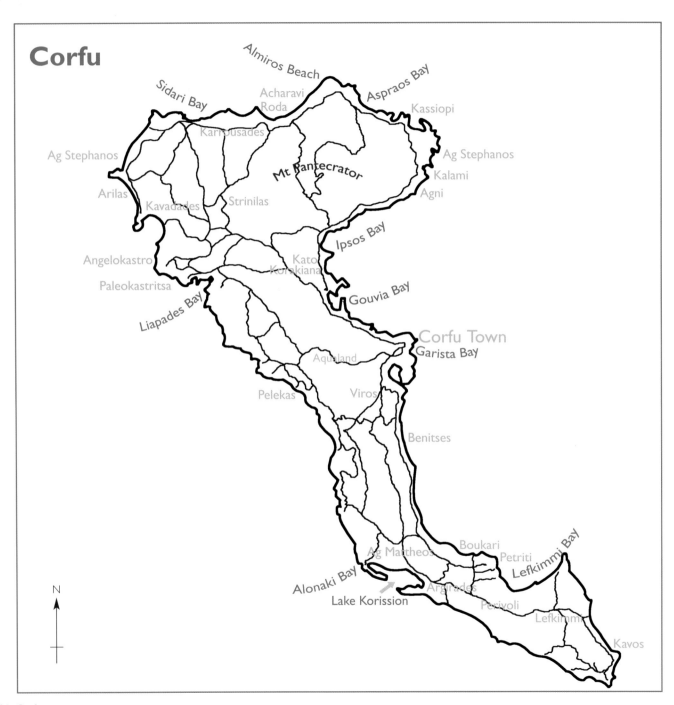

Corfu

Almiros Beach

Sidari Bay

Aspraos Bay

Acharavi
Roda

Kassiopi

Karrousades

Ag Stephanos

Ag Stephanos

Mt Pantecrator

Kalami

Arilas

Agni

Kavadades

Strinilas

Angelokastro

Kato
Korakiana

Ipsos Bay

Paleokastritsa

Gouvia Bay

Liapades Bay

Corfu Town

Garista Bay

Aqualand

Pelekas

Viros

Benitses

Boukari

Ag Mattheos

Petriti

Lefkimmi Bay

Alonaki Bay

Anaplades

Lake Korission

Perivoli

Lefkimmi

Kavos

N

Acknowledgments

Producing a culinary guide, I have discovered, is not a solo effort; it relies on the enthusiasm and generosity of family, friends, friends of friends, and people I never met before but who are still more than happy to help. Grateful thanks to everyone, in particular:

In the UK, Isabel Lloyd, my editor; Emma Borley-Johnson at Speed Management and Lisa Caswell of 2g Ltd, who designed the book; Vassa Challess, who checked my Greek spelling; Elizabeth Dawson, for her industry know-how; and Keith Richards' encouragement and contacts.

In Corfu, Apostoli and Min Kazianis, Christos and Anthula Serakinos, and Vasiliki Boletsi were all very generous with their recipes and advice; Nic Kormaris was happy to explain all the different types of local fish and their Greek names; Joseph Silvanos and his workmates were willing to be my 'white mice' and assess the results of my recipe testing; Kate Eales and Stacey Flanagan were an excellent source of taverna recommendations; Philip Parginos provided insight on olives and herbs; Angela Papageorgiou was very helpful with local business contacts and advice.

And last but not least the Bennison family: my parents, Hugh and Sue, for their love and support and for having the very good sense to buy a house in Corfu in the first place; my brother, Jamie, who helped to keep my nose to the grindstone throughout the production of this book; my sister-in-law Jo, who tolerates a family of foodies, and my nephews Henry, William and Robert, who are demonstrating early signs of being gourmands in the making.

Index

notes

135

notes

notes